LOUISE GOODFIELD

Plant Your Grief

100 Poems and Prompts on Loss and Impermanence

First published by Cotton Field Publishing 2025

Copyright © 2025 by Louise Goodfield

All rights reserved. No part of this publication may be reproduced, stored or transmitted in any form or by any means, electronic, mechanical, photocopying, recording, scanning, or otherwise without written permission from the publisher. It is illegal to copy this book, post it to a website, or distribute it by any other means without permission.

Louise Goodfield asserts the moral right to be identified as the author of this work.

First edition

ISBN: 978-1-0686065-3-3

This book was professionally typeset on Reedsy. Find out more at reedsy.com

To the silence...

Absence is a house so vast
that inside you will pass through
its walls and hang pictures on the air

— Pablo Neruda

Contents

Introduction	1
Let's Write About Grief	10
How to Use This Book: The Seven Cycles of Grief	20
Dropping Off The Map (Shock and Disbelief)	30
NIGHT	32
SIREN	33
SWERVE	34
STARE	35
VACANT	36
JARRED	37
SLIDING	38
MISSING	39
GONE	40
DISTANT	41
BLINK	42
WEB	43
Oozing Wounds (Pain & Guilt)	44
WOUND	47
TRAPPED	48
WISH	49
STAIN	50
IMAGINE	51
UNDONE	52
FADING	53

DIZZY	54
CLUTCH	55
TOOK	56
FRACTURE	57
BURST	58
SNEAK	59
BROKEN	60
LAST	61
Throwing Stones (Anger & Bargaining)	63
FIRE	65
SCREAM	66
LIE	67
SHOVE	68
SINK	69
DEFIANCE	70
STUCK	71
WEIGHT	72
BOIL	74
SINGE	75
TRADE	76
WHY	77
The Penny Drops (Depression)	78
LAY	81
REPLACED	82
TAKEN	83
FALLING	84
FLY	85
NEVER	86
FLOODED	87
HUNTED	88
REACH	89

BLACK	90
BURIED	91
INERTIA	92
The Veil Lifts (The Upward Turn)	93
LETTER	95
OPENING	96
LIGHT	97
RARE	98
SMILE	99
SPIN	100
MEET	101
FRIEND	102
RELIEF	103
STEP	104
ALLOW	105
Construction Site (Reconstruction & New Pathways)	106
PROMISE	109
SIFT	110
STRETCHED	111
LEARNING	112
EMERGING	113
REFUGE	114
PROCESS	115
DIFFERENT	116
TRUST	117
HELLO	118
FLOAT	119
REPAY	120
FLOW	121
POSSIBLE	122
TOWARD	123

BLOOM	124
DECISION	125
FORWARD	126
MEANING	127
Living With Loss (Acceptance & Hope)	128
BRIDGE	132
SHIELD	133
SURVIVED	135
SAFE	136
SOFT	137
IMPERFECT	138
LIFT	139
DESTINY	140
INDEX	141
BEGINNINGS	142
TIDES	143
FLEETING	144
LIVING	145
THANK	146
RAINBOW	147
READY	148
CHANGE	149
REMEMBER	150
AFTER	151
Afterword	154
Acknowledgements	159
Professional Grief Support & Resources	162
About the Author	166
Also by Louise Goodfield	168

Introduction

Give sorrow words; the grief that does not speak knits up the o-er wrought heart and bids it break
William Shakespeare

Wherever there is life, there is love, and within the act of loving and being loved—there is also loss and grief. Over the years, I have come to understand grief as a process of learning. In the initial stages, it's like trying to interpret a language I've never come across before. There is a period of shock when I realise I can't communicate—I expect to understand its sounds, syntax and tenses immediately. I doubt my own capacity to endure long enough to figure things out, and succumb to pain from stress and the fear of the unknown. Then, there is intense frustration and anger at myself, others, and even God for creating such a language in the first place. After that, comes the despair and hopelessness which causes me to shut down completely. I think to myself, *I might as well never speak again because no one will ever understand me.*

Then on some insignificant day, the squiggles on the page become sentences—they start to mean something. I begin forming connections and making progress I never thought was possible. All of a sudden, my confidence grows as I gather my experience and begin to decipher the discoveries. Then—just when I feel like I'm on top of things, the language changes in an instant and I'm a beginner all over again.

Learning is a never-ending process and when it comes to grief—it's messy, messier than death if I may say, as death is so final. Beginnings and endings overlap each other in a continuous cycle, and just when we think we're finding some sense of clarity, we are thrown into turmoil once again. Thankfully, the opposite is also true—just when we feel that the pain will never end, a ray of hope appears in the darkness. It is this process, however painful—that teaches us compassion and empathy for others. Through this journey, we are better equipped to support those who have only recently come to know the foreign language of grief.

Throughout my life, which has been heavily littered with loss—I had one tool that supported me more than any therapist, friend or distraction. It was expressing my grief onto paper. Writing my feelings down, and having a space to scream, soothe and regulate was incredibly healing. The page listened without judgement, offered me a release, and allowed me to stay in conversation and connection with myself—even if I was isolated from those around me. Even now, writing never ceases to offer a way for me to articulate the enormous and complex emotions that are whirling around my mind, body and spirit.

However, there was a time when I had no idea how powerful the act of writing could be. I used to spend so much of my life trying to avoid the pain that grief brought. I was determined not to let my past define me, and I was so fearful of being a victim, that I pushed it all down into a deep part of myself. I didn't want to be pitied, I didn't want my life to be a sad story. You hear life coaches exclaim—*create your own story and be happier! Don't identify with your story or what happened to you, decide who you want to be...* and the list goes on. I was ashamed and judgemental of my story and so I abandoned any correlation I had to my past. My story had become my greatest fear, and my darkest shadow. The most damaging aspect about all of this wasn't the numerous losses and heartache I'd experienced in my life, but that I was carrying on as if they weren't affecting me.

Even within the journey of writing this book—I had been grappling with how much of my personal story I should share. *Who am I to write about grief? Is this self-indulgent?* I got so worked up, I decided to give up on the manuscript for a time. Then I came across the book *On Grief and Grieving* by Elizabeth Kübler Ross and David Kessler. It's a follow on from the well-known book, *On Death and Dying*, by Elizabeth Kübler, which first coined the five stages of grief in 1969. In the preface of *On Grief and Grieving*, David writes that Elizabeth—who was coming to the end of her life at that time, told him, *'you will have to go into grief yourself, if this book is to become all it should be'.* This line haunted me for days. I knew she was talking to all of us out there who have the tendency to bypass the more raw and vulnerable aspects of life. It was after this, that I reached out to a poet, a very prolific poet whose poem on grief has lived under my skin for some years.

I realised that if I couldn't continue with this book as it currently was, as *I* currently was—I had to take a different approach. I had no idea how to contact this poet, I had never asked a poet for permission to print their poem in a book before and it was way out of my comfort zone. *Do I contact her agent? Does she have one? Will she think I'm mad, or worse, an amateur?* I did a Google search and found a very precarious contact email address that I assumed was inactive and I took a punt. I felt compelled to resist the urge to persuade her, to prove that the book or I was worth it. Something came over me and I surrendered to a feeling that I simply must ask.

She emailed me back the next day saying I would be most welcome to use her poem in the book. That was incredible in itself, but what made my heart flutter was her sharing with me the curious timing of my email. She explained that the email arrived in her inbox on a very important date—the birthday of a family member that she had lost in recent years. I went outside into the garden to process what had just happened, when the sky greeted me with what looked like an open door in the clouds. Bursting through were golden rays of light illuminating the horizon as far as the eye could see—it was breathtaking. I shared this experience in my reply to her and she said that this moment had the air of 'gift' about it. I felt so too, and took it as a sign.

This was a small but stark reminder of the omnipresence of loss and grief. Her sharing this vulnerable truth with me, took all of the objectivity and distance out that I had feebly tried to hold onto. This connection between us, helped me return 'the why' for this book. I realised that I do not write this book because I'm an author, I write it because I'm human, and if there is one thing that the losses in my life have taught me—it's that there is no wrong or right time to go deeper into grief because life is cyclical, happening all at once and we are forever saying goodbye. If I can make one person's journey a little lighter by sharing my story, then it's worth the risk it took to get here. I know it's not easy and I understand it takes a lot of courage to face our pain—that is why I thought it would help if someone else goes first.

Your greatest gift lies in your deepest wound
Unknown

I was born into a volatile home where I watched my parents slowly lose their battle to alcohol addiction. My Dad rarely showed his love or any emotion except for anger when he returned home from the pub. My mum drank for various reasons but a big part was to manage the anticipatory fear, stress and to cope with a life that was unsafe and unpredictable. I was grieving the loss of a safe loving childhood before I even had the opportunity to experience what safety was, that mixed with the childlike notion that this was how everybody's parents were, I had no idea as to the damage that it would cause later on in life.

When I was twelve my Granddad died and I was put in a car with a bin bag of clothes. My mum and I moved to another part of the country to look after my Nan. My Dad and brother didn't come with us and I felt sad leaving them behind. I innocently hoped this would be the end of grief and a life lived in constant fear, but it only compounded in other ways.

My Nan passing was the first time I stood in a room with death.

My mum wasn't home, she was drunk and at the neighbour's house. I will never forget the look in her eyes when she returned and realised what was going on. Pure terror and guilt. I can't imagine how she must have felt afterwards, I didn't have the words at that age to comfort her—I could only stare wide-eyed at the paramedic trying his best to make her heart start again. A piece of me left at that moment, and never returned.

I didn't have many friends to confide in about what was going on at home. I was bullied for most of my school years which chipped away at my self-esteem. I felt unable to invite most people around our house for fear of unpredictability at home and even though my Mum did her best to keep calm and carry on, every day I lost her a little more.

So when the opportunity to be free of watching in hopelessness arose, I ran headfirst into it. I went to university with no idea how vulnerable I was, how my childhood had affected me and how it would continue to do so. Desperate to belong, I threw myself into a throng of hormonal teenagers who initiated me into the student drinking culture. As a result, I suffered numerous psychological and physical traumas after getting involved with a group of troublemakers. On the plus side, I loved studying drama, which became extremely difficult to concentrate on when my Dad had a stroke in my second year, and later died when I was twenty-two.

After graduating from university, I was determined to make a go of being an actress but experienced constant issues with stable housing. My mental health took a nose-dive and I was homeless at twenty-six. My self-worth was continuously stripped away due to a string of abusive and incompatible relationships that I was attracting in. I had no reference to what a healthy relationship between people looked like.

In 2018 I was living with a narcissistic boyfriend in London when writing showed itself to me as a way to work through and release the grief piling up inside me. I had gone to the doctors (because that's where you go when you are sick, right?) and he was dismissive, almost annoyed. After just ten minutes, he waved his hand and said I had generalised anxiety (which I would find out much later on was actually a misdiagnosis of ADHD). I left feeling deflated and baffled, I had wanted to be fixed and had pinned all of my hopes on this appointment. I knew if I left the GP's surgery at that moment, everything that was becoming so painful and wrong in my body would continue to get worse.

A quiet voice inside of me was whispering *you deserve more*. So I sat down, pulled out a notebook and pen from my bag and began to scrawl a deluge of words onto the page. All of the unanswered questions, anger, worry and frustration came pouring out. I let my grief bleed in ink for reams and reams. That out-pouring became my first ever spoken-word poem, titled *Sick*. It was the start of a long journey of learning how to claim my life back, the one I felt I had lost out on.

I would love to say that grief then went off to live with someone else and I lived happily ever after, but this was just the start of my story of finding a way to navigate loss. It took many years and everything I had to arrive at a place where I could write this book. Admittedly, I was scared of what the writing process could unearth. I would have to face the darkest parts of my grief if I was to ask you to do the same, and was I ready to do that? Is anyone ever ready to do that? Working through this book myself—I became ready.

As I have shared my story in increments over the years, both verbally and on paper, I have come to befriend it. It has made me courageously soft, compassionate, and highly sensitive to the emotions and needs of others. It has enabled me to go on a path of healing and to then offer compassion for those who need it most. Expression has been a bridge to understanding and the way home to myself, which is why I believe it has the power to save lives and why it saved mine.

Has it made me the ultimate expert on grief? Absolutely not. The moment I feel I get to grips with grief, it opens me up in entirely new and unexpected ways. However, it has been enough to help me wade through tumultuous waters, foster resilience, and shine a light where I can. While you may not have come across this book with the intention to help others, writing is an invitation for those with their own difficult stories to know that they aren't alone. By living your truth and sharing your story, you will have a massive impact on the lives of those around you.

If you are worried about the brevity of what I've just shared with you, or if you are concerned about opening old wounds because of the fear you may never return—I not only survived my story, I thrived. I unpicked the myriad of emotions and released that which no longer served me. I talked to grief, to my loved ones now gone, honoured my painful experiences and arrived at a place of gratitude and acceptance for where those losses have led me.

So whether you are seeking solace, a mirror to your own pain, looking to create your own body of work around this theme, or simply trying to figure out how you feel—this book will help you connect with your grief, write through the toughest and most vulnerable moments of your life, and find hope on the path towards living with loss. There is room for your grief here. These pages will not abandon you or become freaked out by the turmoil going on in your inner and outer world. You deserve to be seen and known, and your story is truly a gift.

You aren't going to be thrown into the deep end without any tools to support you either. I'm under no illusion that you may be new to expressing your grief through poetry or prose or some other form. So in the next few pages, I will be offering an insight into the many ways available to you when it comes to writing grief down, as well as how to get the most out of this book.

In the face of such heartbreak, what else is there to do but turn to the page and write for our lives?

Let's Write About Grief

There are some griefs so loud/They could bring down the sky/
And there are griefs so still/None knows how deep they lie
May Sarton

When someone says, 'let's write about grief', or another multi-faceted concept, it can be overwhelming to try and articulate something that takes years to understand or experience fully, especially that which we would rather avoid. The good thing is, no one is asking you to do that here, we can leave that to the scientists, the experts and the non-fiction writers to come up with thick tomes on the topic. What I encourage is expressing your grief and your experiences with loss in your own unique way. I invite you to open your heart and put pen to paper, without letting the worry of what may surface stop you from sharing your truth.

Thankfully—there isn't only one way to write about grief. There are so many unique versions to be made out of us being here on this earth, and the tiniest, most inconspicuous detail within a memory, can open up a world of understanding, connection and healing.

For example, *Grief is the Thing with Feathers* by Max Porter is a novella about grief narrated by a crow and tells the story of a grieving writer and father of two young boys who is coming to terms with his wife's death. *The Long Goodbye*, is a powerful memoir by Meghan O'Rourke following the aftermath of her mother's battle with cancer, *Self-Consciousness* by John Updike offers personal reflections on the mortality paradox, and *The Wild Edge of Sorrow: Rituals of Renewal and the Sacred Work of Grief* by psychotherapist Francis Weller provides rituals, reflection prompts, and deep wisdom for healing and renewal.

Writing about grief doesn't have to be all doom and gloom or esoteric either. There are a fair few humorous books, essays and poems centring around grief such as *Griefstrike! The Ultimate Guide to Mourning* by Jason Roeder, a finalist for the 2024 Thurber Prize for American Humor and a best comedy book of the year, or the novel *A Man Called Ove* by Fredrick Backman which has now been turned into a movie on Netflix, starring Tom Hanks.

If you are a lover of non-fiction and like to get to grips with the science behind the 'why', *The Grieving Brain: The Surprising Science of How We Learn from Love and Loss* by Neuroscientist Mary-Frances Connor PhD blew my mind and reframed my thoughts around grief. The OG on this topic is Elizabeth Kübler Ross, who first coined the 'Five Stages of Grief'. Her book *On Death and Dying*, has helped millions of people give a name to their experiences and understand the inner workings of a topic often pushed out of public conversations.

Letters have also been a trustworthy confidante to the most

intimate elements of our grief, preserving our love and pain dutifully in its pages. They are a time-tested way to express that which we can't quite tell our loved ones face to face. Irish author, poet, and playwright, Oscar Wilde for example, wrote a letter to his close friend and lover, Lord Alfred Douglas, after his imprisonment in Reading Gaol. The letter was titled 'De Profundis', which in Latin translates to 'from the depths':

> *For us there is only one season, the season of sorrow. The very sun and moon seem taken from us. Outside, the day may be blue and gold, but the light that creeps down through the thickly-muffled glass of the small iron-barred window beneath which one sits is grey[...].*

Similarly, the musician Nick Cave wrote a letter to a woman called Cynthia who had asked him a question on his website about his late son:

> *I feel the presence of my son, all around, but he may not be there. I hear him talk to me, parent me, guide me[...] These spirits are ideas, essentially. They are our stunned imaginations reawakening after the calamity. Like ideas, these spirits speak of possibility[...]Create your spirits. Call to them. Will them alive. Speak to them. It is their impossible and ghostly hands that draw us back to the world from which we were jettisoned; better now and unimaginably changed. With love, Nick.*

Poetry is arguably the most proficient and expansive form in which to translate our experiences of grief to ourselves and others. *Making a Fist* by Naomi Shihab Nye is a wonderful example of how imagery, metaphor and detail can evoke and articulate an experience as vast as grief.

Making a Fist by Naomi Shihab Nye

We forget that we are all dead men conversing with dead men.
 —Jorge Luis Borges

For the first time, on the road north of Tampico,
I felt the life sliding out of me,
a drum in the desert, harder and harder to hear.
I was seven, I lay in the car
watching palm trees swirl a sickening pattern past the glass.
My stomach was a melon split wide inside my skin.

"How do you know if you are going to die?"
I begged my mother.
We had been traveling for days.
With strange confidence she answered,
"When you can no longer make a fist."

Years later I smile to think of that journey,
the borders we must cross separately,
stamped with our unanswerable woes.
I who did not die, who am still living,
still lying in the backseat behind all my questions,
clenching and opening one small hand.

From *Grape Leaves: A Century of Arab American Poetry.* Copyright 1988 by the University of Utah Press. Reprinted with permission from Naomi Shihab Nye.

Naomi expresses the fragility between death and living to the reader vividly. The image of the little girl opening and closing her small fist in the back seat coupled with Naomi's razor sharp metaphor, 'my stomach was a melon split wide inside my skin', makes us not only *see* the poem, but *feel* it too. Whether this specific series of events are fact or poetic license, is unknowable without asking Naomi herself. What is more important is how poetry can be used as a tool to articulate the most complex, and provocative facets of our human experience.

A poem is so personal to each reader. For me, *Making a Fist* brings to life the countless times I spent with my mum in the car going to and from my childhood home in Surrey to Suffolk, where we later lived during my most formative and difficult years growing up. It gives form to the trust and also pain that both my mother and I were going through together and separately. It also makes me curious about all of the life changing moments and revelations that have happened on long-distance car rides and how relationships are strengthened and also broken.

Another poem that you may be familiar with is *Immortality* by Clare Harner. This poem has been recited for generations at memorials and funerals—it has been copied, edited, reworked, claimed by other poets, and was declared one of the nations best loved poems via a BBC poll on National Poetry Day in 1995. In 2004 *The Times* wrote: "The verse demonstrated a remarkable power to soothe loss[…] crossing national boundaries for use on bereavement cards and at funerals regardless of race, religion or social status". The version I have included was published in *The Gypsy*, in December 1934.

Immortality by Clare Harner

Do not stand
   By my grave, and weep.
I am not there,
   I do not sleep—
I am the thousand winds that blow
I am the diamond glints in snow
I am the sunlight on ripened grain,
I am the gentle, autumn rain.
As you awake with morning's hush,
I am the swift, up-flinging rush
Of quiet birds in circling flight,
I am the day transcending night.
   Do not stand
   By my grave, and cry—
I am not there,
   I did not die.

Immortality is a beautiful rallying cry from the other side, and it implores us to *live.* Whilst being frank in its request—there is a hopeful and loving message that all of us want or need to hear, that our loved ones live on, within and around us.

Poems are powerful portals to memory, feeling and experience. They get to parts of us that nothing else can seem to reach. Even if you have never written a poem in your life—I would encourage you to explore what poetry can offer you when it comes to expressing your deepest and most heartfelt feelings—I promise it won't disappoint!

Writers and poets will often use a line from someone else's poem as a springboard for their own. For example, they may start a poem with a line from Naomi's *Making A Fist,* 'I who did not die, who am still living…' or Clare's *Immortality* such as, 'I am the thousand winds that blow'. Personally, when faced with the erroneous task to try and pin down a concept as wide and varied as grief, I like to choose one tiny detail of a memory, and zoom in. I focus on the texture and smell of a scarf someone left in my possession, or a freckled nose I no longer get to look at. Then I choose a one-word prompt to help anchor my writing. If you haven't come across the word 'prompt' before, it simply means a word that is intended to inspire a thought, feeling or memory—which can then be expressed creatively.

The examples above are meant as signposts if you need a little steerage, but a huge part of the beauty of the writing process and of this book in particular, is the space to figure out how you feel. Sometimes we have to start writing from a place of confusion, and reach into the unknown. This means a messy blob may need to come out—not a poem or an essay, but an amorphous blob of feeling and thought. This is normal, and it may have been how Naomi's *Making a Fist* or Clare's *Immortality* first made it onto the page too. All of the examples I've shared have undergone a fair amount of editing and are by writers that have had prolific careers dedicated to their craft, so don't feel that this is by any means a 'standard'. It is simply my hope that by introducing them—they may offer you the spark you need to write your own way towards the light.

So why don't we have a warm-up write together and put some of these elements into practice?

- Write down three memories or moments in your life that impacted you in a big way
- Write down three details that stand out to you when you recall those memories, such as colours, scents or textures
- Select one of those details within a memory
- Use the word TEAR as a prompt (you don't have to include the word in the poem)

For example:

Memories
1. Leaving my childhood home
2. My dog dying on remembrance day
3. Moving to Canada five months pregnant

Details of events
1. Bin bags, carsick, petrol fumes
2. Black curly fur, red tartan scarf, autumn leaves falling
3. Winter frost, deer munching leaves, monster trucks

Prompt: TEAR
After Making a Fist, by Naomi Shihab Nye

I who did not die, who am still living,
watched my childhood try to reach me through
the tear in the black bin bag as we gasped for air—
the stench of cigarette smoke and petrol
suffocating our young lungs.

* * *

How did it feel to write in this way? It is completely normal if it felt clunky and weird and not like anything you've experienced. Unless you write poetry regularly or are an established writer, then it would be a lot to expect you to feel any other way. Expressing yourself through poetry is like exercising a muscle—it will get stronger with use. Notice that I have credited the poem and author of the poem whose line I used in my example above. I normally format it like this—*After [Title] by [Author/Poet's Name]*. If you end up using any of the lines from my poems or anyone else's work, and then decide to share or publish externally—you must credit the original author or poet.

The final thing that I would like to address when it comes to writing about grief is perhaps the most important. I want you to imagine a circle in your mind's eye. This circle represents your capacity to hold the losses in your life. When you experience these losses, this circle splits into segments, fractures, even—but everyone's circle is always the same size. It's the inner workings that are different. Whilst we all experience grief in varying intensities based on our coping strategies, history and other contributing factors, if you are mourning the loss of a new relationship that has gone sour and then someone shares that their entire family passed in a car crash, your grief does not become irrelevant. What is going on within your circle of grief is personal to you—meaning that there is no facet of grief or 'type of loss' that is more or less deserving of love and attention.

If you're feeling like you don't have enough grief to write about—trust me when I say it will surprise you how much pours out when you get started. Often the devastating loss of a pet gets considerably overlooked—or the loss of a culture or a sacred place that was built upon. Even the small daily griefs that we try to brush off deserve acknowledgement—a rejection email, not getting picked for a sports team or invited to a party. It is all relevant. So if you are comparing your grief to what others have lost and its making you feel guilty, or you aren't used to having the time and space to work through and process your emotions—it is natural to feel hesitant.

In that case, I'd like you repeat after me:

It does not matter if I have experienced 'more' or 'less' grief than others. My grief in whatever form, circumstance or timeline is just as important and relevant. I deserve to have my grief aired and expressed. I have compassion for my journey and will not compare, minimise, or allow anyone else to minimise my experience of loss.

Now you have your own permission slip to grieve as loudly and as deeply as you need, let's have a little recap:

- **There is no one way to write about grief**
- **Detail is a useful way to begin when you are stuck**
- **Your grief is no bigger or smaller than someone else's grief—it all matters**

I hope this chapter has offered some useful ways in which to write about grief, now let's have a look at how you can get the most out of this book, and how we are going to spend our time together over the next few months.

How to Use This Book: The Seven Cycles of Grief

Suffering is one very long moment. We cannot divide it by seasons. We can only record its moods, and chronicle their return. With us time itself does not progress. It revolves
Oscar Wilde

You may be familiar with the term 'The Five Stages of Grief', modelled from the book by Elizabeth Kübler-Ross, *On Death and Dying*, which was first published in 1969. The five stages include: Denial, Anger, Bargaining, Depression and Acceptance. However, I will be structuring our journey on the expanded version which includes seven:

- **Shock & Denial/Disbelief**
- **Pain & Guilt**
- **Anger & Bargaining**
- **Depression**
- **The Upward Turn**
- **Reconstruction & Working Through**
- **Acceptance & Hope**

I've taken the liberty of adding my own poetic slant on the original title for each stage, and although Elizabeth never intended for the word 'stages' to be limiting or linear in any way, stages can signify reaching somewhere at a specific point in time and in a particular order, which grief does not adhere to *at all*. Cycles however, can be repeated and have no clear end or beginning—so I thought that was a better fit.

In any case, it's not too important what they are called, the priority is for us to find some common ground and allow us to explore the various shades of grief that we have all experienced, so here is my adapted version that we will be writing through:

- **Dropping off the Map (Shock & Denial/Disbelief)**
- **Oozing Wounds (Pain & Guilt)**
- **Throwing Stones (Anger & Bargaining)**
- **The Penny Drops (Depression)**
- **The Veil Lifts (The Upward Turn)**
- **Construction Site (Reconstruction & Working Through)**
- **Living With Loss (Acceptance & Hope)**

I understand that this may not be the order in which you travel through your journey of grief, so please feel free to delve into whichever cycle first calls to you. Each cycle includes a series of one-word prompts with original poems. Each prompt is clearly marked in capital letters at the top of each page with the title of the poem in bold underneath. Each page will be structured like this:

(Prompt) SAVED

(Title) **When I Was Least Expecting You**

(Poem) If I knew how to swim…

It is my intention that you would turn to the first prompt within the first cycle on the day you want to begin and write without editing or trying to make it perfect. However you can also run your finger down the contents page and pick out a prompt that speaks to you on any particular day. This is not about following a curriculum, but letting grief speak as it needs to. This is your journey—you may be going through more than one cycle at the same time and my suggestions are simply an offering to help get you started.

You may wish to pick one particular experience such as the loss of a loved one and write about that the whole way through the book, or you may wish to engage with the myriad of ways grief has impacted you and see what each prompt will bring up for you on the day. Whatever you decide—reach out to one person in your household and share with them what you are undertaking so they can support you. If you live alone, a neighbour, friend or mentor who can check in with you to see how you are doing is an important resource to have during this time. This seems like something that is easy to skip but trust me, you will be glad you did when you find that you need them.

You can absolutely use this book to help develop your own poetry collection or memoir on grief. Writing daily fragments or poems is a great way to help you build some coherence in your writing practice and encourage momentum. If you are feeling stuck on what to write, I'd recommend that you compile a simple list of the moments of loss or impermanence that have occurred in your life or return to the 'how to write about grief' section of this book.

I would recommend purchasing a journal, notebook or diary specifically for this journey. This will help you to keep everything together and make it easier for you to return to when you need to. Google Drive is also a helpful place to save and store your work online if you prefer. It is a free cloud based system so your words are protected and saved automatically as you write. Personally, the act of writing by hand is more of a somatic experience for me, and I tend to write more deeply from the heart that way—but it is up to you where you put your words.

* * *

Spending ten minutes clearing off one shelf is better than fantasizing about spending a weekend cleaning out the basement
Gretchen Rubin

Before we get to writing, I would like to share a method I have been using every day for years. It has been the most compassionate and gentle practice I've come across and has supported me through imposter syndrome, writer's block, procrastination and many other moments of self-doubt. The method is simply to set a ten minute timer and write on a one word prompt that day. The timer helps to avoid overwhelm or hyper-fixation, it makes the writing manageable and gives a little dopamine hit when that alarm goes off. It sounds painfully simple, but it takes the pressure off before, during and after the writing.

This method is designed to be flexible, and the prompts are just a starting block. Grief, as we know, does not have a stopwatch—so if you are in the midst of making a breakthrough or you're getting to the heart of something, keep going. You may need some time to process and give yourself some rest between the various cycles, you don't need to write on a prompt every day but if you feel like you are on a roll, follow that feeling!

If you don't write every day when you had planned to—forgive yourself. When that happens to me, instead of beating myself up about not writing or telling myself why I'm so rubbish, I simply love myself back on track. That will mean different things for each of you, like going for a walk, returning to why you wanted to speak your grief in the first place, or listing the benefits that will come from your expression. It may even be to reach out to a friend for encouragement, or asking your spirit guides, or loved ones now passed for their support.

This ten-minute method got me writing, but I would not have kept going had it not been for the community of writers across the globe who joined me in writing one poem a day for the past two years. This took place most notably within the wonderful Facebook group created for the readers of my first book, *Plant Your Poetry: 365 Poems and Prompts to Grow Your Writing Habit*. It was a place for them to share poems with each other and with me. It was transformational for so many of us and it was within this group that I began to understand the true power of community, of being witnessed and held in our experiences. I am thrilled to be offering a similar space for readers of *Plant Your Grief*.

I will be showing up daily for the first one hundred days to offer live readings of the poems, write with you on the prompts, and offer you support and encouragement throughout this journey. You are welcome to join and introduce yourself from the moment this book lands in your hands, but the group will officially open on the 22nd September 2025. I hope these testimonials from those who joined the Plant Your Poetry group will offer you the assurance that you will be well cared for:

> *"Louise, you have created magic here, and my sense is, have opened so many hearts to possibilities we may not have even noticed. Your gifts overflow. Thank you so much for your feedback in such a profound and loving way. I hope you know how much you help people on this page by reading what we write, and responding the way you do. You are the shining example of how all teachers of poetry should be with their students/followers. You are amazing!" - Jack*

> *"Thank you so much for your words. I actually wrote out what you'd said onto a post it note and stuck it onto my notice board as a motivator for when I need 'inspiration'. If you're wondering what you are, you are a whole hearted mentor to every contributor within the PYP community. You've added so much value to my writing habits." - Eliza*

> "I can't begin to explain how important this group has been and continues to be! You are all amazing and I can't wait to connect further with you all." - Brooklyn

> "I have written a poem every day since this book was published, growing my personal writing practice and enjoying interacting with other writers through Louise's Facebook group. I discovered I had purchased much more than a book! Membership of this community is a daily balm to my soul." - Jane

To access the group, scan the QR code on the back cover of this book, or go to Facebook and type *Plant Your Grief Community* in the search bar. Within this group, you can connect with others and share your responses to the prompts if you feel comfortable to do so. You don't need to worry about any of this right now if you just want to start and see what happens—but it has always been my intention that the *'Plant Your...'* series will offer you much more than a book. The greater purpose is to offer opportunities for connection, community and transformation in some small or big way.

A little note about the poems I've written alongside the prompts:

I hope the poems will offer solace, companionship and inspiration as we travel these one hundred days of writing through grief together. However, if your expression doesn't look like the poems I've written or like the examples I've shared previously in the book, please know that doesn't mean what you have written is wrong or bad. My poems are not intended to be examples of what you should be writing and they have been edited to provide you with an excellent reading experience. You may not want to write poetry at all, you may want to journal or begin to gather the fragments of a memoir. There is a very real chance you've no idea about any of that, in that case I would encourage you to just get to the first prompt, feel it out and practice seeing where it leads.

I will repeat this again because it's super important. Do not concern yourself with writing *well*. Our inner critic or editing hat will worry about that much later down the line. Just write *now* and know that it can be done, and that you are the one to do it.

Where necessary I have included content warnings for each poem but if you find yourself struggling with the subject matter or a particular prompt or poem is triggering in any way, I have included professional resources and helplines at the end of this book. It may be a good idea to have a look at these before you begin. You can also decide to move on to the next prompt and poem and leave that one indefinitely, or return to it later.

So to recap:

- Turn to the first prompt within the first cycle on the day you want to begin
- The prompt is the single word in capital letters at the top of the page
- Use these prompts to support your own poetry collection or memoir on grief—or to simply figure out how you feel
- Set a timer for ten minutes and write without editing as

you go
- If you are feeling stuck on what to write, return to your list of losses and hone in on some details
- Scan the QR code on the back of the book or search 'Plant Your Grief Community' and join our supportive Facebook group
- This group will provide you with the details on how to join me for a free writing workshop on grief
- You don't have to write poetry, write in whatever form you wish—even if there isn't a name for it
- Tell someone you are working your way through this book so that they can check in and support you
- There are professional services and resources at the back of the book should you find any of the content, poems or journey triggering

Final note:

This is not a book revealing new scientific information about grief. It is an invitation to help unlock emotions that are stuck in your mind, body or spirit. It is a message from my heart to yours: *you are not alone.* I will not tell you what grief *is*, but I will support you to explore what grief means to *you.* The personal stories before the start of each cycle are intended to offer food for thought, and to illuminate. I am not a grief counsellor or a psychiatrist by any means—I am a poet simply offering a springboard for your own discovery. In doing so, it is my hope that you can express, release and reveal yourself. Care has been taken at every moment to make sure that this book is valuable, inclusive and safe to those navigating grief.

I invite you to stay curious and to treat yourself with kindness. Any emotions that arise are valid, and part of the process of learning to navigate life without what or who was once on your personal map. It can be a reassuring thing to know that just as everyone learns at a different pace, so do people grieve and grow on their own timeline. There is no positive or negative cycle, so lean into it all. Remember, your story is a gift—you are safe and you can do this.

Shall we begin?

Dropping Off The Map (Shock and Disbelief)

*They are all gone into the world of light,
and I alone sit lingering here*
Henry Vaughan

I was at a friend's house having a meeting with my company when I received a call from my mum—a family member had committed suicide. I remember hearing the laughter from around the table in my present reality and the strangulated silence from the person on the other end. Suddenly I was neither here nor there. I was floating in a dream, like I had been untethered from the Earth. My brain flailed around trying to make sense of what I had just been told. I felt like a statue as I put the phone down and repeated the words that had been said to me. It didn't feel real as it came out of my mouth. My body shifted into auto pilot and we continued with the meeting. There was no crying or beating of the chest, but the air was different—heavier. I retreated into a small part of myself and became painfully aware of how many eyes surrounded me. I wanted to shut them all and unravel alone, but instead I sat there and we all carried on as if nothing had changed.

In the *The Grieving Brain: The Surprising Science of Grief and Loss*, Neuroscientist Mary-Frances O'Connor mentions that our brains are hardwired to be able to locate our loved ones from a blueprint created in the brain over a long process of repetition and habit, which works like a map. When that loved one or thing suddenly drops off of that map, by choice or unwittingly, the brain *can't* fathom what is missing. It's not that we don't like the truth or refuse to believe it—our brains are dumbfounded, reeling from the nonsensical information it has just received.

This cycle often occurs in the immediate aftermath or even during losing something or someone. The prompts that follow will help you articulate your own experiences of what I have just shared with you, or perhaps they will uncover something else—in any case, go gentle on yourself, take a deep breath, and write for your life.

NIGHT

The Black Womb

In the black womb of night
I am alone. The whites of my eyes
punctuate the featureless shadows
as I writhe in agony on the bed,
hands clutching stomach,
begging the Gods of The Void—
Please don't let it be the baby.

The house is silent
except for my ragged breath
as panic begins to creep out
from under the covers.
I reach into the nothingness
and fumble for a light switch.

It is all I can do to send a text
into the ether in the vain hope
to be witnessed, to feel close
to someone. I grab a book,
let the author offer comfort
and try to last the night.

SIREN

Make Way for One Who is Mortal

The siren sings across the city: *Make way for one who is mortal.* A reminder that life is not ours to play with, but that we are the plaything. We guard life as if it were the point, that in death we cannot live—but aren't those closest to death the most alive? The siren is mute, its sudden absence of song lords loudly in my ears, everything fades to black...

SWERVE

Trying to Join You

I am in the middle of the road
and the traffic is swerving around me,
clipping my clothes as I sink into hot tarmac.

No one has time to stop.
They beep their horns so loud
I can't hear your voice anymore.

I am trying to join you—
hoping they'll file us away together,
bodies tattooed with the same paved road.

But there is no impact—just a gush of air.
I'm being maneuvered around so fast, life blurs
into a mirage I cannot name or touch.

STARE

They Won't Know I've Left

Time stops. Or is it my heart?
Blood rushes to the surface of my skin.

I want to be alone so my face can fall
through the centre of the earth—

everyone is staring at me and so
I must be bones holding up flesh.

I dig my heels into the ground
and look them straight in the eye

(So they won't know I've left).

VACANT

An Empty Hollow Where Wonder Used to be

The world is provoking me out of my shell. Every look is a dig, every vague question I don't have a good answer to wounds me. I can't recall sights and sounds that once brought me peace. When did the vibrance of colour fade? This is not me, but an empty hollow where wonder used to be. My vacant body lay frozen in a ceremonious casket, I'm a mere echo of all I have endured.

JARRED

The Laugh That Erupted from Her

Heart racing, pen jarred between page and hand. I can't stop thinking about what just happened—her brow furrowed to a severe meanness, body twisted, half threatening, half completely ridiculous and the laugh that erupted from her without a smile—a jaw opening and closing like a ventriloquist dummy.

SLIDING

I Have No Hands in Which to Catch You

I have no hands in which to catch you
from sliding away like soap suds
on a slippery plate.

I am not God. I am not the Tree of Life
or the Four Horsemen.
I am a Sunflower

that lives and dies with the day—
nothing more than a mirror
to the sun's orbit across the sky,

blooming when you rise,
and withering when you set.

MISSING

No one is Home

I am searching for you in the supermarket,
on the bridge, at the dinner table,
even at the music festival—and you are missing.

Your soul has been squeezed into a tiny corner of you,
I want to shake it out before we lose it to monsters
neither of us are big enough to fight.

No one is home anymore—your eyes glazed
and your conversation culled to a few agreements
whilst people drum a dance on your skin.

You are sullen and sulking—I beg you,
before its too late, before you do not recognise
real from not real.

I cannot bear to watch this happen, not to you,
after everything you have overcome—
all that I love, *please come back to us.*

GONE

Popped to the Shops

The breakfast congeals in the pan
and your water spills over the cold glass,
pressed into my hands as if the taps would run dry
the moment you walked out the door.

As the day stretches the laws of time,
the house utters sounds that I don't recognize—
but the bells comfort me with their familiar ring
as they honour lovers departing and returning.

You're not gone—you've just popped to the shops.
Yes that's it. Our future is translucent, a shy bride.
I shall sleep for a month and wake up in your arms,
the breakfast eaten and the glass empty.

DISTANT

A Snail With no Shell

I can't see two feet in front of me. Everything has lost its meaning. Familiar faces are now foreign and language fails me. People open and close their mouths but the words aren't words they are just sounds too distant for me to hear what is actually being said. I'm floating away on a cloud, God has saw fit to remove me. What was wrong with my old life? I am a snail with no shell, salt, everywhere I turn.

BLINK

Knee-Deep in Bodies, Muck and Blood

It happens so quickly. That's the thing about time, we spend so much of it preparing, that death is upon us before we can blink. It does not live in the past or future, and that is always where we are looking for it. Then we are left looking at the entrails, mouth agape—holding the pitiful wrinkly balloon-like skin of our lives.

We spend our days reliving the attack, trying to pick it apart— knee-deep in bodies, muck and blood. The debris piles so high we're encased within a labyrinth of our own making. After many excruciating days spent kicking the walls as a means to escape, we get on our hands and knees and start digging.

Tears come and carve the quickest path as we follow the water to lower ground. But wait, wouldn't we be better off hiding here, where we'd be harder to find? We stay—and grow used to the blood. Yesterday's battle becomes tomorrow's fortress.

WEB

Demolition Man

It's not just the loss of a singular body—but the shattering of a web of a life. Schedules, impulses, patterns of speech, plans made and unmade, obliterated with a heavy *thwack*—like a child who has decided to play demolition man with a spider web. Now a big fat nothing lies between two points of reference. The language we've spoken for years has become extinct overnight. Our house has been dropped like a pin in an alien city whilst we were sleeping. We try to go about our day but everyone acts strange and talks only with their eyes which they arrange into a frown/smile/grimace that imitates that they understand, but how could they? Their house is in the same street it has always been, their web of life intact and shining from the early morning dew.

Oozing Wounds (Pain & Guilt)

Pain is the great teacher of mankind.
Beneath its breath souls develop
Marie von Ebner-Eschenbach

Before I moved to Spain, some of those I considered to be my best friends, signed a document for my voluntary removal from a theatre company we'd built from its inception. Seeing those signatures felt like my heart had been torn in two. I thought of all of the times where I had gone out of my way to help them personally and professionally. I wanted to confront them of course, but I felt that any efforts made to stand up for myself would be seen as confrontational and would only contribute to their vilification of me, and of course—there was no neutral HR department to bring my concerns to.

None of them reached out to me after to see how I was in relation to their decision. I cried every night for weeks with all of the conversations that I was unable to have with them going round and round in my head. Perhaps this was only a business decision to them, but they were my friends first and foremost. I couldn't change their narrative, even though I felt a searing sense of injustice. I felt so strongly that their perception of me wasn't at all who I really was. I was back home staying with my mum and was due to be going to live and work in Spain in a few weeks. This should have been a moment of triumph for me, instead I felt like crawling up into a ball and disappearing forever. My trust in people was completely shattered. More than anything, I felt rejected by the few people I would have lain down my life for. My heart was crushed and the pain was all-consuming.

Loss is often out of our control, but even if we have initiated it—self-blame, shame and guilt can rear their ugly heads. We want to fix the problem faster than we are able to, and we start to question whether it was our fault that things went wrong. Thoughts such as, 'I should have called them', 'I should have known', or 'I should have been there more', become repetitive self-inflicted wounds in our psyche. There is an intense desire to change the reality as it stands in the present moment and this causes deep emotional, mental and physical suffering. It's not just that we can't get over a loss or that we are too sensitive. Our brains are trying to find out *why* something feels wrong, and the longer time goes on, the pain and frustration from not finding the problem can intensify.

Like tensing up before a blow or crash, our bodies want to protect us and so we shrink and cower, bracing for a blow that is so huge we can't even see it. Another element of this cycle may not be the obvious arrival of pain, but the numbing of it, whether external or internal. We often turn on ourselves in these moments, it's easier to blame ourselves when the object of our pain or loss isn't around to direct our hurt at. This is a time where everything seems to hurt. It's like our body is constantly oozing blood. We can't think straight, we can't function and it gets harder the more we try to rationalise. We either fall apart and don't shower for weeks, or we go completely numb. We mask as best we can but the wound is deep.

Use this cycle to confess and pour out your pain without worrying about being 'dramatic' or reacting too much. This is your space to air your sorrow and fear, to pull them from your heart and throw them across the page. Allow for tears and for questions with no answers. Lean into the pain. Imagine that whatever your truth is, you are going to be perceived with love and understanding. As Khalil Gibran emphasised, y*our pain is the breaking of the shell that encloses your understanding.* This raw pain is movement—so take a deep breath and pull out those thorns.

WOUND

There is Nowhere That Does Not Hurt

I was born a wound that attached itself to a body—why else am I this way? There is nowhere that does not hurt or that does not want to hurt me. I just want somewhere to go that does not rub, and live there forever. I must return to the place I was made—my mother's womb. I will crawl back in and try to arrive at a different time.

TRAPPED

One for Sorrow

I'm more at home with the wild birds
than with humans. They speak a gentle language—
a curious glance, a tilt of the head
and then back to plucking worms from the Earth.

Meanwhile, a child thwacks her baby brother
so hard on the back, that the impact entangles itself
like a butterfly trapped within my ribs.

The magpies swarm and protest alongside me—
one for sorrow, two for joy, three for a girl,
four for a boy.

WISH

Your Second Skin

I love you and I wish we spoke more. I wish you'd call and share snippets from your day. I miss you so much that when you do call, I want to tell you all about the grief and the missing parts of my life I'll never retrieve—but I accidentally knock over the dog's food bowl and swear as if I am too busy for this. You retreat like a hand on a hot stove, feeling like you've caught me at a bad time, but it's all a bad time at the moment—I'm a bad time.

I wish you'd call more, I wish it even as I'm talking to you on the phone, there, now. I wish I was a blossoming rose when you do, and not a mussel shell clamped so tight there is no hope to prise it open. Perhaps that's why you don't call much—you think I'm busy, or annoyed.

I'm trying to keep busy to stop wondering when you are going to call and then I ruin it by pretending to be aloof. Which never works—you pushed me out of your own body. I am your second skin, there is nowhere in this world where we are not born from each other. Still—I wish you'd call more.

STAIN

Can You Grieve Something You Hated?

That red mattress—its canvas worn and threadbare at the edges, sagging around metal spring curls that bullied my skin. The white and orange sofa emanating a faint whiff of urine, their forlorn cushions tattooed with brown burn holes. The big grey settee, where I would stretch out sick with flu—mum's perfumed coat blanketing me. The upturned fire grate, laden with random items I would sell whilst playing shops. The space between the settee and the cabinet that hid a scared little body. The huge table that creaked as if it were still a living tree. The fish nobody wanted that lived longer than any of us expected.

The thin rattling window between me and the moon. In all of her phases I loved her—I always knew where she would be.

IMAGINE

To See Her Eyes Light Up

I imagine her death a thousand times.
Sometimes I long for it—in that I see no other way
for the pain to stop. When it finally does happen,
I will spend my days bringing her back to life.

She'll park herself in her brown leather chair
and down a coffee whilst complaining of a headache.
She'll watch the soaps on the highest volume setting,
and phone me, shouting her words over the noise.

I imagine her death a thousand times,
but what I really long for—is to see her eyes
light up one last time. In death I can do that,
I can put the light back in her eyes myself.

UNDONE

My Skin is a Blanket of Buttons

My skin is a blanket of buttons flailing open,
catching the light and clipping each other.

Far from home, they crave their openings—
no one to put them back where they belong.

Hanging,
   waiting,
     will I ever feel properly clothed again?

I have been brought into this world
to be undone.

FADING

When She Can No Longer Sign her Name

When she can no longer sign her name,
I won't keep the birthday cards with no trace of her,
with a perfect rhyming message that she decorates
with speech marks as if they are spilling out of her mouth.

I'll keep the post-it notes hidden inside my lunch box,
I'll keep her declining signatures, the ink barely
tiptoeing across the page. I'll keep her words alive
by reading them aloud whenever a room gets too quiet.

DIZZY

Content warning: Loss of a child

Dizzy With the Love my Body Can't Contain

A burgundy rose deflowers into the bowl, my pee is the colour of flushed cheeks or a lip stain—the love is pouring out of me. I search the still pool for answers, dizzy with the love my body can't contain and wait to feel her move inside of me. My body cries pink tears and I do not know who for or why. I suffered, this body changed itself from the inside out, I carried, I hoped, I washed and scrubbed and still, still she may not want my body for a home, still it may not be enough.

CLUTCH

The Gap That Begins to Swell

The mother clutches her two young boys
like babes in each arm on the family sofa—
taunting my empty ones.

I hug a yellow cushion to try to fill out
the gap that begins to swell—if I was
swallowed whole, they wouldn't notice.

Under her wing—they're invincible,
the way she ruffles their hair,
puts a stopper on death.

TOOK

Lost Together

It took him one minute to steal my heart—
his stare boring into me behind filmy translucent lids

are you my mummy?

It took me two minutes to see myself reflected in this
fledgling orphan, filament-thin skin scorching in the sun

are you my brethren?

It took five minutes to wrap him gingerly in my white
cotton cardigan and carry him to my apartment

we can be lost together

It took thirty minutes to become an expert on birds,
and start romanticising about our new life together

my shoulder will be your home

It took him two hours to fall asleep on my finger,
for me to wish I was the size and weight of a penny too,

people might take more care with me.

I daren't close my eyes in case he needs me.

FRACTURE

Lunch is Over

There is never enough time to fracture—
for splintered fragments
to hurtle through membrane
and lodge with significance.
No time to swell or bruise,
no room in the office
for splaying stomach first
on the carpet,
hands full of *them,*
clinging and despising—
we must get back behind the desk.
Lunch is over.

BURST

I Long to Put Her Into a Deep Sleep

I've tried to pinpoint what is eating her from the inside
but her laugh is loud and bold enough
to shoo my suspicions away for a while.

Her eyes—when she perceives she is not seen—
are large orbs, swivelling to catch everything
before it smashes to the floor.

I inhale deeply to remind myself that there is enough
oxygen in the room for everyone as she storms
around the kitchen going red in the face.

I long to go to her and put her into a deep sleep—
let her rest like a newborn in my arms,
but she fights to keep a lid on everything.

She thinks I'm worried that she isn't okay.
It's not true—I fear she may burst
and wither on the floor of this kitchen,

mouth opening and closing,
muttering unintelligible words
like a goldfish out of water.

SNEAK

See You Tomorrow

You always hear poems from those
who never got to say goodbye,
but what about those of us who did?

We are oceans watching stones
drop into our bodies to the tune
of an over-zealous gulp.

Children gulp loudly when they're
pretending to be afraid. That's because
the last goodbye is make-believe at that age,

but still they stagger down the aisle
in the supermarket with a toy trolley,
screaming for their lost Baby Born.

It's an Oscar-winning performance,
but no, the last goodbye is quiet, and tries
to sneak away from the party via the backdoor.

Of course my Dad's last goodbye was a joke.
I don't remember the setup, but I do remember
the punchline—S*ee you tomorrow.*

BROKEN

The Hardest Part

I can do without you disappearing off the face of the earth, which isn't really a face, but a large scrap yard—a kid kicking a ball again and again at a fence on the inside of my brain, *not again.*

I can do without a conversation that has no point or end but trips over itself and gets stuck in the names of people I've never met. I can do without my basic grid being broken, you stumbling around snagging joy with your fingernail, trying to waft away your cigarette smoke as if you suddenly care about our health. Telling me I should be grateful as I am broken over and over again.

It isn't your fault and that's the hardest part. There is nobody to blame but the elusive shadow that devours your light. We are never far from what will consume you in the end and I'd love to say I can do without you but I can't, please God—I can't.

LAST

I Never Thanked You

I sit here in the white dress that you urged me to buy for a fiver in a charity shop. You were adamant that I had to get it. As I stroked its smooth fabric covered in small birds in flight—we had no idea they would fly me across the ocean and down the aisle.

I stare at the crumpled white veil I rescued from a mummy bride in Value Village with no idea how to attach it to my head and I know who I need. I think of all the times I've been openly annoyed at you for doing *mum* things—ironing my socks, buying me things I didn't ask for a week or so before I actually need them. Like those size 12 cotton pants when you found out I was pregnant, which I reluctantly stashed in my suitcase at the last minute just to please you.

That was the last gift you gave me before I left, and I want to tell you—you were right. Like when it poured with rain at the local music festival and you rushed from home to give away all of my coats to sodden and sullen teenagers. You were soaked and dripping, and all I could do was express my deep embarrassment.

I am about to get married on the other side of the world and you aren't here. I wouldn't accept your help if you were, but you'd find a way to be intensely involved, as you always did—something I never thanked you enough for. I lean over the steam from the iron and try not to melt the veil. I'm trying to learn to do it on my own, which turns out—is much harder than you made it look.

Throwing Stones (Anger & Bargaining)

At first grief feels like being lost at sea: no connection to anything. Then you get angry[...], the anger becomes a bridge over the open sea, a connection from you to them[...] It is something to hold on to
Elisabeth Kübler-Ross & David Kessler

I am not quick to anger because of years of conditioning that this emotion is shameful and not something that women should feel or release. It is harder to recall a memory where anger was my main experience. But I have screamed myself hoarse underwater, into a pillow, in the shower and at the top of a cliff. I've banged my head against walls, dug my fingernails into skin and ground my teeth so intensely that they were in danger of cracking.

I have sat in my breeze-block lined tiny room at university, in the midst of chaos after upturning most of my possessions. I felt like a pressure cooker full of steam that had no where to go. My insides hurt and I couldn't think or see clearly. Throwing some things around was the lightest outcome of how I actually felt inside—like I was about to explode.

Anger and bargaining are common bedfellows with pain and guilt. This cycle can often feel like throwing stones at a river trying to make it hurt as much as we are, but the stones just sink and we've only managed to wear ourselves out. Throwing stones doesn't seem to do anything to change the circumstances, but that doesn't mean expressing anger in a healthy way is wasted. It's an important part of the learning process. Just as shame thrives in the dark, so does anger, and anger suppressed can surface later on, in more dangerous and damaging ways.

If suppressing our anger stores the grief deeper into our bones, how may we convey and release that anger through image, colour or text? What does being angry feel like? If anger was an object or a colour, what would it be? What words can we use to grow closer towards articulating the heat emanating off of us? What would we say to the universe or our loved ones if we could give them a piece of our mind? Being angry in this cycle doesn't mean you will stay angry forever, this is a safe place to rage, to not take the higher ground, to stop trying to grieve perfectly or keep yourself in check. So take a deep breath—and erupt.

FIRE

The Silence

A heavy steel clap threatens to crack my skull,
my blood is on fire and the silence is the worst of it all.
I've decided it's okay if I don't last the day.

SCREAM

No One is Coming to Save Us

The cicadas are angry. They scream from the trees as the wasps float silently, their bodies limp and lifeless on the skin of the water. Who knew that water could lure us to our demise, when the Earth is scorched dry and the world is thirsty? How to know what is quick safety and a slow trap?

A wave builds inside me and spills out across the shore of my mouth, I submerge and wail within the watery wasp graveyard. There is nothing I can do but make bubbles no one will ever see. No one is coming to save us.

I spot a sign of life, grab a shoe and scoop a sodden yellow and black body out of the water. I watch it stagger away, strength building with every step. I stare up at the sky, wave my arms and wait to be scooped.

LIE

Your Eyes of Cool, Clear Glass

I dreamt about you last night,
and your eyes of cool, clear glass.
We bumped into each other in town
and you let me stroke your forehead.

You caught my eye for the rare occasion—
and there was so much love between us.
We told each other that we still cared
and that we always would.

I also dreamt that Prince Charles
was shot dead by a man on roller skates
dressed as a beefeater, and then I remembered—
you haven't spoken to me for months.

SHOVE

The Most Important Work

I am alone in the park, sinking my teeth
into cherries and guzzling lemonade,
when a boy of three squeals with delight
at the proximity of a baby bird eluding
his outstretched hand. He follows a trail
of magic that only he can see—when suddenly
frantic arms push, and shove
his wriggling limbs inside a pram.

He squeals in protest
until he is limp with defeat,
the most important work of his day
left unfinished. The adults don't see—
the flowers blooming at his feet, the pixie dust
from his mid-adventure kissing his skin.

His mum pushes him unceremoniously
to the dedicated 'play' area. No plants,
grass, or birds, just tarmac pretending to be sand
and plastic pretending to be trees.
She leaves him in the pram—in his cell,
and the void grows behind his beautiful eyes.

SINK

The Thrill is Always Down

Bodies become distorted flesh in the sands of time, boats can no longer stay afloat patched up by the sailors trying to find their way out and then home. Mud squelches underfoot, groans—must we always try to build our flurry of desire on this? All that sinks is okay with itself—we were never part of the grand plan—and now all that wants to leave must try to creep out the back door, unbothered. But we have tethered ourselves to the roller-coaster, where the thrill is always down, down, down—we crave the plummet whilst blaming the motion for the fact we can't get off.

DEFIANCE

We Will Exist
After 'Moonrise' by Gerard Manley Hopkins

Desperate for sunrise, I sneak
a knife-flick peek at the black box sky.

Eyes searchlight the crumbs of stars,
fingers grasp my umbrella like a lance

as the moonlight hits its metal tip
illuminating a smiling gift on the gravel.

I carry the grin of a thin white fingernail
into the white and walk of the morning.

Who knows if we will ever return
from our walks these days?

I pocket our kin's epitaph—
they will not erase all of her.

We grow defiance
in our wombs—we will exist.

STUCK

I Pay my Taxes and my Dreams Shrink

Paperwork does not work. Does not agree with me being British and free to work in Spain, does not agree that my Dutch husband and I should be together in the same country for the birth of our baby—who could be born in Spain but wouldn't be Spanish, or born in the UK and wouldn't be a European. Paperwork wants me to remain stuck between the multiple choice, because when I am stuck—I pay my taxes and my dreams shrink until I am cold and dead in the ground.

WEIGHT

The Great Pacific Garbage Patch
A gyre of marine debris particles, in the central North Pacific Ocean. The collection of plastic and floating trash originates from the Pacific Rim, including countries in Asia, North America, and South America.

It was made
by those
who are dead—
the weight
of five hundred jumbo jets
three times
the size of France
and the dead,
with belly ache—
keep it.

It was made
by those
who are dead—
immortality
for castaway crates and
stateless plastic flesh
which drift
towards the shores
of our metered lives,
until the time comes
when

there are no shores
and all drown
in the weight
of five hundred jumbo jets
three times
the size of France

and we
the dead
with belly ache—
eat it

singing
our shanty song:

it's too much

it's
too
much

we
are
full.

BOIL

Bronze Rage
After a bronze of 'The Damned Soul' by Massimiliano Soldani-Benzi

How is it that rage
has been moulded onto a man's face,
only to spurn him *Damned?*

I glare at the imbecile who states
*men can't help themselves when it comes to women—
it's in their DNA.*

I want to smash his head through the table,
but when have you ever seen a punch up
in a poetry workshop?

I scream into my steaming mug,
resembling the bronze bust pictured
on this postcard.

I wield my pen and boil his foul mouth placid,
pummel sinewy chest, and crack his eyeballs
into their sockets.

I reach into his genome, extract his DNA,
strip each strand like the leaves from corn,
and devour them raw.

SINGE

Food Chain

Grief is not for the dead but for the living, to know there is still *a living*—a life trapped inside every object and person that loses all colour and meaning to us for a while. It is a torch about to be lit, an attentive match, a pot put on the stove while we decide what we have the energy to put in.

It's also the cold side of an edge that cracks our shell open and leaves our insides out on the counter top. The yolk has no time to catch up before it's tossed onto the heat, sliding around for a while with no form or edge. It thins until the edges begin to singe and curl so the rest knows where on the food chain it lives. The moment an egg is laid—it's already dead.

TRADE

Death is Not a Politician

What I wouldn't give to trade for more time, to have another chance to say or do what I feared. I want to be a merchant—buying and selling time in warehouses brimming with clocks. But time cannot be sold to the highest bidder—it is an independent body, run by a force indifferent to the whims and fancies of the population. Time is not mine to own, those who have lost a loved one in the folds of the day know there is no select button, no drag and drop—you cannot hold a cursor over a grave and revive them with the click of a button. We are simply wheels rolling down different sized hills. I don't want to be. I want to be the grass at the bottom of these hills as the wheels soar right over me, bursting into beautiful fireworks. But Death is not a politician. Impervious to persuasion—he can't be petitioned or bribed. He's the most reliable friend I have, and I would kill him in his sleep if I could.

WHY

Lab Rat

All I could think whilst in agonising pain was *why we do it to ourselves*?

Why choose a bodily experience if our souls are pure consciousness? How can they have more to learn? Do souls have levels of awareness too? Or do they just need something to entertain them, a way to spend eternity other than floating in the void, bored and finished?

I can't tell you how many times I've begged for this to be my last trip. Which of course, is my body talking. It all feels like an experiment, I'm just a lab rat, and if they love me, then the pain must be preceding something utterly transformative, *right*?

The Penny Drops (Depression)

There are no windows within the dark house of depression through which to see others, only mirrors
Miriam Toews

I fell into a deep depression in the Winter of 2024. At just five months pregnant, I had moved to a new country that wasn't what I expected when I arrived. I got married without any of my family and friends present and could barely leave the house due to freezing temperatures of around minus thirty degrees.

The night before my wedding I was admitted to hospital with severe dehydration. This visit cost over one thousand dollars, and on top of that, I was refused pre-natal care because I didn't have a healthcare number. There were no midwives available and my mobility was limited due to a serious fall down some stairs which shattered my confidence on my feet. That coupled with some huge shifts in my life, as well as living in an apartment with my in-laws who I'd never met before, it is an understatement to say I was going through a considerable amount of stress.

It was one of the toughest times I've ever experienced. Everything I hadn't had the time to process, every hidden wound and unhealed trauma from my past crashed into me all at once. My husband was incredible, yet we were still getting to know each other. I had to learn how to surrender and let someone take care of me, which goes against everything I had ever done in order to survive. I feared for my baby, how could I be a mum if I felt like this? I was a shadow of myself and fell far—so far, I thought I would never surface again.

The only thing that kept me a functional human being in my darkest days was the accountability I felt to show up for the community of writers working their way through my first book, *Plant Your Poetry: 365 Poems and Prompts to Grow Your Writing Habit.* I had promised to show up for ten minutes every day and write live on the prompts to inspire them to keep going. It turns out that this is also what inspired me to keep going, as well as the knowledge that a life was growing inside me.

The last thing we may feel like doing when we are in the depths of depression is to write, and sometimes, it's all we feel we *can* do. 'The Penny Drops', is a time of realisation that no matter what we do, life is passing through us with such intensity and velocity that we are unable to hold onto it. This hard truth can often manifest as feelings of hopelessness, or seemingly feeling nothing at all whilst also feeling utter despair.

Our brains realise that no matter what we do, there is no living the life we once were, with the people we were once connected to. We are stripped of everything we once identified with, and while this feels like a relentless nauseating roller-coaster ride in the dark, it is also the falling towards an edge. Rock bottom becomes something to push off against. Cesare Pavese said: *The only way to escape the abyss is to look at it, gauge it, sound it out and descend into it.* So take a deep breath, remember that you are safe, and let the shadow self in.

LAY

Now is the Time to Give Up

Lay down your head and spill everything the world is too busy to listen to. Let's lay here together until all of it blows over and there is nothing to worry about, nothing to leave or cling to. Now is the time to give up, give it up, lay it down—leave it up to the clouds and by the clouds I mean *everything* as if it isn't taking a part of you with it. Let them make new shapes with what you thought would never change.

REPLACED

Why Does the Ice-cream Taste Like Ash?

Whilst scooping Lego with a tiny hand out of a dusty red box, staring at the pick 'n' mix, eyes closed mid-lick of ice-cream on the beach—everyone around me has been replaced by an actor. Has the sky always looked so full of tears? Was my hair always this thin? Was there always a pain here? Why does the ice-cream taste like ash?

Strange voices intermingle with my husbands mouth, I can't make meaning from the sounds. I feel like a child lost in a crowd. White lights brand the backs of my eyelids, drilling into my brain. I'm stared at intensely as I fall backward in slow motion, away from everyone.

TAKEN

Nowhere To Go, Nothing Left

When there is stark presence of life, it reminds you of what was taken. Where life does not or will not grow, where the fields are barren and the earth parched, when you are so tired of absence—that going down the stairs, opening the door and lying in the road seems like the only logical step when there is nowhere to go and nothing left.

FALLING

The Thud That Never Comes

I will be falling to the end of my days. Feathers are struck out by friends that stall my descent for a while but there is still that groundless, stomach somersaulting panic—nothing to stop the thud that never comes—just a cavern carved around my useless body, nothing to snag me to a slow tumble, just black blinking back.

I fall for so long I grow used to zero-gravity, and it no longer feels like I'm moving at all, in fact, everything seems to fall out of *me* like sewage out of a pipe, everything that matters—gushes away. Where to? The deepest lake that lives nowhere, where fish do not swim and nothing can be caught.

FLY

A Place Where It Is Safe to Rage

Little bird, there on a branch most high, chest puffed up—bracing against the wind. I see you. Just because you have feathers does not mean you have to justify why you're afraid to fly. Wait a while for temperance to drive the storm to a place where it is safe to rage.

Little bird, I see you tilt your head, claws gripping the branch so tightly. You do not have to show me that you are a bird—save your energy. Forget about the crows, you do not have to justify why height gives a bird vertigo, just because you were born for flight.

Little bird, I'm going now, fly or don't. But know that you have just as much right to this tree, even if you fall from it. You do not have to fly, just because you can. Sometimes it's not as easy as wanting or choosing to. Sometimes wings just won't work.

NEVER

A Place Where Never is Always

Never say never they say, and that means all things are possible. Like the fact that there are places you can never return to—childhood homes, lovers, family members or parts of yourself. We can never go back, if back were a time or a place or person, whether we should or could or would—we cannot.

So where do we go now? A place we have never been before. A place they never were, an empty place except for the painstaking existence of my own self, alone.

FLOODED

A Sinking Heart

Imagine you are taking a bath and an unknown force at a random time draws you under, a rush of water fills your ears and mouth, which opens agape like a stunned Koi carp. Your arms feel like ten ton weights—as you struggle to reach for air, willing Poseidon to take you as faces and shapes blur above the water.

Imagine that you notice every single bubble floating from your airway but cannot say what song they carry to the surface as you become lost in their slow dance, and watch with a sinking heart as they burst before they reach it.

Imagine that the water quells as quickly as it began, rushing down an invisible plughole as the topside world moves beneath you again. Imagine you spend the next week trying to catch your breath whilst treading water, striving to not be last, pretending like nothing has happened—like you weren't drowning.

Imagine not being seen or heard from for months, and that no one has particularly noticed—they are too busy clapping the super-human speed at which you front-crawl toward an invisible finish line, legs pumping twice as hard to make up for the weight attached to you. A weight that you can't time nor tame.

HUNTED

Nowhere Left to Run

The dog paws at the door and will not quit. My stomach clenches at the sound of claws scraping wood. A friend or therapist might suggest I open the door and let him in, but I know what will happen. He will eat everything that moves—jaw ungodly wide and ravenous, with hungry beetle black eyes. I am being hunted. It is only a matter of time before he finds a way in—and there won't be anywhere left to run.

REACH

You Need to be Held

Let me hold you like I know
you need to be held.

Let me reach you—allow yourself
to be reached down there in the depths

where you sit and try to prove
that no one is coming for you.

BLACK

The Black House I've Become

Would you stick around if I show you the black house I've become? My own soul a ghost rattling the windows, messages of madness scratched into the wallpaper, pleas that will never see the light of day. Discarded wrappers and broken glass litter the floor—would you dare to pick through and ingest the melancholy spores into your lungs?

I ask you because I cannot escape. A house can't move itself into the fabric of another because it doesn't like its room-mates. I will slowly disintegrate into these four walls. You are better off away from here, unless you are willing to join me. And isn't that what we all fear the most—that darkness is infectious?

BURIED

Until the Bees Carry my Sweet Soul to Someone Else

My heart is a halfway motel with no windows and doors—the seasons pour in and when they leave, they never take all of their detritus with them. I could close up shop forever, but I just want to be buried deep—become a seed that forgets its need for the sun and sleep until the bees carry my sweet soul to someone else.

INERTIA

I Can't See Them Because They Are Enormous

I haven't spoken to her since Marty died—I still feel the compression of his cocktail sausage sized body squeezing my own for warmth, clutching me like I was a life raft in the deep blue ocean.

The grief stricken days go by and the inertia festers. I couldn't save little Marty, I killed him because I cared too much. I have fading hope for myself but I'm still here, clutching onto—what? Perhaps there is someone holding *me* in the palm of their hand and I can't see them because they are enormous. I can feel them feeding me intermittently, keeping me alive—*for what?*

The Veil Lifts (The Upward Turn)

*Someday all you will have to light your way
will be a single ray of hope and that will be enough*
Kobi Yamada

I'd not long returned to London after splitting with my partner. I had tried to start again, renting a room in a house share that I couldn't really afford. I was battling with a deep depression that began way before we separated and every day was a mountain I barely had the energy to climb.

One morning I was particularly melancholy. I felt that life could be more than this but I didn't know how to go about getting there. I felt so stuck and miserable that I went for a walk and ended up in the park on the corner closest to my house. It was a small man-made park and quite uninspiring, but I couldn't believe my eyes when I saw them. Pears! They were overflowing from a *wild* pear tree, growing audaciously where it probably shouldn't have been. This small moment was such a surprise, it shocked me out of my lament. I gathered some in my hat and rushed home to wash and poach them.

I could relate to that pear tree, it gave me hope that perhaps I too was full of promise—that despite my environment, I could bloom. That evening, full on the sweetness and excitement of change, I wrote a sentence that seemed inconsequential at the time, but possessed a power that accelerated my healing journey over those next few years. It was: *I commit to life.*

When the veil of grief lifts, there is a lightening to the darkness that *would never end.* The intensity is what begins to lessen, or at least, elements of life that were once solely good, that lost their flavour alongside grief, begin to gain their vitality again. You may notice you've laughed hard twice this week without wanting to tell them about it. You heard their name mentioned and didn't feel physically sick, or you returned to that hobby you had before grief robbed the joy out of it, if only for a minute. It could be making your first homemade meal in a while, responding to a text, or maybe it is the moment you find some wild pears in the middle of London and start to feel hopeful again.

The prompts and poems in the next few pages offer a space for you to tap into these minuscule moments of lightness. This isn't to say that grief is over, there is also a lot of confusion and guilt about being happy, or forgetting some things you vowed you never would. But it is a single unencumbered breath, the trill of birdsong, it is relief that something has shifted. Even if we can't identify exactly what that is, it gives us just enough strength to carry on. So take a deep breath, lean towards the light, and lift the veil.

LETTER

There Will Never be Enough Glitter in the World for Everybody

Dear You,

She eats everything in the fridge, sleeps on your side of the bed and steals your clothes from the wardrobe—which she never intends to return. She uses up all of my makeup to cover her bags and now empty bottles and brushes lay discarded. She soaks my cushions until they're mostly water and hosts parties to forget, to feel—to escape. I clean up after her without a word and comfort her when she tells me *there will never be enough glitter in the world for everybody.* I make her tea, of which she only ever drinks half.

On the first day of Spring, she laughs—chases butterflies around the garden until she sees me looking and covers her face with her hands. She writes me a letter—it says she has found another place to live, that she can see her company takes its toll on me, and that she is strong enough now to move on. She says that I can have her side of the bed. I go upstairs to the bedroom—a ton of glitter scatters the pillow.

Yours forever—

OPENING

The Room is Not Full of You

A sliver of light creeps through a crack in the door. Last night it was closed shut and I've no clue whose hands did this work—I live alone. There is a gentle breeze caressing my cheek, is it Spring already?

I notice with a start that the room is not full of you. You must have seen the small opening and scarpered. I wasn't holding you captive—I just knew you'd leave given half the chance, so I kept all of the windows and doors shut. I've been sleeping on the remnants of all you left behind for months, but now there is new furniture—furniture that you probably would have hated.

A kettle tuts in the distance and I hear two cups clinking as they kiss. I stare at the sun's rays reaching over to me through the open window. We haven't seen each other in such a long time. I reach out and let them caress my skin.

LIGHT

A Long Way From Home

Two shapes of light dance at the edge of my bed. They arrange themselves into figures, one the size of a child and the other an adult. I do not feel in danger—just a long way from home. They don't say a word, but their presence speaks to me. I feel a father-like energy, a father who has let go of anger and left it to rot on Earth. From the child, I feel pure love. Perhaps the child was my sister who I never got to meet, who died just thirty minutes after she was born. Their company calms me and I fall back asleep like a child soothed after a nightmare.

RARE

Two Cups

I opened my eyes this morning
and didn't see yours blinking back at me.

My body didn't curl around the imprint
of your body in the memory foam mattress,

only when I padded downstairs
and clicked the kettle on did I begin to ask

do you want a cof—

It had taken a rare twenty minutes
to realise you were gone.

I made two cups
in celebration.

SMILE

Where All of My Sorrows Swim

I forget the night sky is empty of you until you return—a curved smile of light on a black lake where all of my sorrows swim. I remember this too is a phase, that time passes, or I pass by time and her checkpoints—that I'm not alone, that I survive to speak with the dark side of the moon and all who sit in her shadow.

SPIN

Normal People are Shy and in Love

I spin the globe, the entire map of the world swirls before me, and I am stuck in a tiny part of it wishing to drop off entirely. I'm sure in the yellow zone there is some kindness though, in the green, a woman has decided to treat herself to two pastries. In the orange, two normal people are shy and in love. In the blue, there are whales singing to each other whilst a calf is born. I try to let it all become the *bigger picture*.

MEET

Heavy Metal Concert

A single tree meets the storm. Its branches—arms held up in ecstatic prayer—wave to a single rose in the far distance. The rose moshes so violently I worry its neck will snap. All around me, nature thrashes around at her own heavy metal concert but it still feels rooted, and brave. My bare feet are planted on the earth, my hair reluctant to join the throng. I pull a blanket tight around my shoulders.

Nature is unbothered and unapologetic. She continues to remind me how to shake a stick at the storm. Music arrives over the heavens and rains her quartz and quavers on my skin. I can do nothing but join her. It is no longer clear where I end and she begins.

FRIEND

Everything She Is

Are you okay? This is not a throwaway line, this is a flung rope in the unforgiving sea. I don't know how or where to begin—but then, it never *begins* does it? Suddenly you are in the middle of it all, thrown in the deep end, treading water for your life.

She is younger, yet surveys me with acute attention as if she has been watching over me every day since I was born and can read my thoughts like a sprawling map. She doesn't speak—but with everything she is, she says:

I got you—as I'm drowning

I got you—as I'm pulled towards shore

I got you—as my feet find sand

I got you—as water spills out of my stomach

I got you—as I take my first breath in what feels like months.

RELIEF

Sweet Nectar

Relief is such a quiet guest,
I barely notice her until I catch myself
humming whilst hanging out the washing,
inhaling a stunning mountain vista
whilst the sticky juice of a nectarine
runs between my fingers.

I slide my tongue across my chin
and relish the sweet nectar
of not having given up.

STEP

A Series of Small Things

Like the lining of a stomach,
or the bottom of a well, there is
an edge to grief. When you get here,
it's a surprise—it seemed as if
the nauseating fall would never end.
Yet—rough stones smooth with time,
rivers run dry, civilisations rise and fall
and so grief too—has it's orbit.
Every year is a series of small things
that make up for the grief, that fill
the chasm with a fresh breath—
as we take a tentative step forward
on the lonely swing bridge
between the ages. Each time
our foot connects, we hope that
by carrying on, we'll find another,
and we do—*we do*.

ALLOW

It is Time

A robin perches to drink,
a deer's tail bobs between
the trees in the distance

and every single pine
bears the weight of snow
with a hushed humility.

I sit by the windowsill,
and allow my empty hands
to find a paintbrush.

I press the hairs
into the condensation
on the glass.

It is time to start
another painting.

Construction Site (Reconstruction & New Pathways)

The struggle you're in today is developing the strength you need for tomorrow
Robert Tew

Shortly after publishing my first book, I decided to visit my Mum to get some much needed 'home' time. We had been getting on well, she had even come to visit my husband and I in Spain for her birthday. Returning was a stark reminder of all of the pain and fear I'd felt as a child, watching my mum succumb to alcohol addiction I was plunged back into an old pattern and lifestyle that I had almost forgotten existed. My nervous system freaked out, I was genuinely shocked at how quickly this wound surfaced and I could feel all of the work and healing I'd done since I'd left the UK unravelling before my very eyes.

I couldn't believe I had lived for years pretending as if everything was normal. I didn't want to enable her drinking any more. This was no longer about me trying to convince her to stop, but about me giving myself some much needed self-care. For years I was worried that if I drew away from her it would make her worse and I felt responsible for her emotions in many ways. I returned to Spain adamant that I would never stay with her again. I was disappointed and annoyed at my naivety. Somewhere deep within me I had always thought: *this time things will be different.*

I realised that moving away and engaging in my own personal healing could only do so much. This experience had happened to show me where there were still wounds in my life that needed attention, of grief that was still in my bones—desperate to teach me something. Ironically, I became pregnant that same month, and although I wanted nothing more than to be close to my mum at this particular time in my life, I had to make the heartbreaking decision to cut ties. I separated us from an invisible soul-contract I had felt compelled to keep since I was born, one that had been doing long-term damage to my mental and physical health.

This loss felt like I was ripping a hole in the fabric of time and I felt every inch of the devastating absence. My world as I knew it was caving in. Grief and guilt were inescapable, not just for me—but for my daughter too. I was no longer bigger than my grief, or busy enough to bury it and I had no choice but to let it in. It was this that propelled me to end a lifelong cycle of pain and separate myself from a wound that was never mine to carry.

I will always love my Mum, she did some incredible things and cared about me in ways that went above and beyond. She was never a bad Mum and I have so much respect for her and everything she went through. I would never wish to punish her. I only hope that one day she will reach out to someone and receive the help she deserves. When writing this book I contacted her and asked for her blessing to publish parts of my story so that I may help others going through similar things, and she gave it. Things do seem harder after healing in the short-term, but the foundations that are laid by making a different choice are so much more secure and necessary in the long-term.

This is a clunky and messy phenomenon, much like a construction worker building a new skyscraper from the ground up, there are blueprints to be drawn up, skills to acquire and materials to be ordered. We have to figure out step by step how we are going to go from empty space, to a solid building—from wobbly legs, to sure footing. This can take so much longer than we anticipated and can feel like we are taking two steps forward and five steps back.

However, it is a time when certain aspects begin to make sense again. The world is no longer a pile of rubble. We are beginning to clear the debris to make way for something new. It can be nerve-wracking to let go and leap into a life without grief as the most dominant aspect in our lives, but there is a small voice that says *keep going*. Each step, each brick we lay is a commitment to a life we deserve. We keep on living as a way to honour all that we lost to get here, which paves the way for who we will become. So put on your hard hat, take a deep breath and start building.

PROMISE

The Last First

At just seventy millimetres big you move within me like a promise, or the day before Christmas. You with your arms outstretched over your head, legs crossed like you are chilling at the beach, know nothing of grief.

I'm your biggest fan the moment you make your first appearance on the big screen and I have to remind myself that you are not mine, that I will have to let go tiny parts of you every day. Every first will also be the only, and last first. It makes me determined to keep my eyes on you—my total eclipse of the sun. A rare celestial occurrence that could blind me in an instant, and yet I still can't look away from.

SIFT

The Nature of All Things

I've knelt with my knees in the mud
sifting for gold through rooms of the past,
some that were built long before I arrived.

I've been sifted too—a small grain of sand,
carefully and cruelly inspected in a palm
to be chosen or tossed back toward the angry sea.

Why sift through thousands of grains of sand?
There must be something else we were destined for—

perhaps to crane our creaking necks
toward the horizon and just *empty our pockets.*
Kick it back into the nature of all things

and let the grains grow smaller—
polished by the burgeoning distance.

STRETCHED

Old Summer Bones

Tears sail the aches away, sobs swim out
from the undercurrent and try to dislodge

the lingering winter
from these old summer bones.

My body bucks like a bull at the rodeo
trying to get out of and yet keep its skin.

I am being stretched from the inside out
and there is nothing to be done, except

sweat out what is no longer my life.

LEARNING

Let Everything Hurt

My life has exploded and I'm not sure whether to spend my days scouring for each far-flung severed morsel, or to simply start learning to live without a shell—let everything hurt for a while. Barefoot, bare-skinned, my entire body like a sensitive tooth. I'd grown used to being numb, but this is what some people call *being alive.*

EMERGING

In the Wild

I stumble out from the hazy days spent in the wild,
exposed, open—a target for every high root and low branch.

As the landscape steadies, shapes slowly draw into focus
and the trees whisper, *only a little farther to go*.

Have I really grown as resilient as they tell me? Wide-eyed
and terror struck, my heart wishes to cry a thousand woes

but all I have seen has left me bereft of language—aching
from the effort of travelling to the edges of myself.

And then I see the future galloping toward me
like a wild horse—I ready myself to meet it.

REFUGE

What We Never Had

Is it strange to see a building as a friend,
and is it true that one can find sacredness
or refuge anywhere—even within one's own body?

*Sometimes we don't need to be pushed out
of our comfort zone, because we've never been
inside of one.*

PROCESS

All at Once

There is no day when grief does not run her fingers through my hair. There is always something that is in the process of leaving and let's not forget the grief that arises when grief itself returns, and we mourn the laws of life itself.

I had not always known this. I thought grief had picked me out of a line-up and decided, *that one will suffer,* marching me off to the sub bench away from everyone else. I thought I was born into this world to take the hit, soak it up like a sponge—and I did. I never thought about why or what comes after. I never thought a person could carry a loss that does not minimise their love or joy. That a person can feel *everything all at once.*

DIFFERENT

Something I've Never Tried

I am trying not to picture your large, helpless and reproachful eyes—pursed lips cracked and thinned. I am not in the business of leaving you but somehow I've become an entrepreneur and the investment isn't looking good. What am I saying? This isn't business, this is family, and it hurts like hell to be leaving you.

Yet it was never my test—I am going halfway across the world and even though it feels like pulling teeth the farther we are from each other, the distance will never be enough to erase all that percolates between us. I think about you every day and I wish things were different. Instead *I* have to be different, this is something I've never tried. To plant my own life. The mother in me must say goodbye.

TRUST

I'm Not Yet Meant to Know Such Things

Spirit whispers that I'm not yet meant to know such things but simply answers that I am safe. *I trust you*, I say, hundreds of feet up in the air, floating between the clouds. We enter into a comfortable silence until a small mouse-like squeak of doubt emerges from the depths. I am still unable to believe that I am here for what they say I am.

As if to answer my secret question, my earphones—snugly asleep in my ear—burst into song. It is a song that is halfway through its play on Spotify, which wasn't open. As if in a dream I hear: *I've got another page in my book and I will use it well, I will use it well, and when I go, I want to know, that I left it all on the table. That I gave it all I've got, I wanna be remembered as love, leaving behind a legacy of light.*

I let the words sink in as we begin to descend, leaving parts of me scattered across the ocean. I thank the her that brought me here, but she cannot go where I am going now. That is the way of metamorphosis.

HELLO

Until the Waves Grow Kinder

Hello is a long slow-motion goodbye that connects you to another time and place, like building a boat, pushing it out onto the water and watching it sail towards horizons you will never see.

It isn't easy, sometimes the sky can be as black as velvet and the tides grow choppy and testing—hiding all from view. But the boat will always exist, causing ripples at new harbours without you as a captain. Persevere until the waves grow kinder. Storms would never be storms if they didn't pass. One day the boat will return to you in some other sea and you'll be so proud of the journey it took—and the stories it will tell.

FLOAT

No Care—Just There

In this poem I imagine I am the cloud I see
from the corner of my bedroom window.

I do not wistfully cling at parts of myself,
there is no thought, just float, no care—just there.

I am not opaque, others can see through me
if they reach out their hand and swirl me around.

I dance between their fingers and follow the flow.
When it's time for me to go, I simply get moving

in the sky's own time and witness my form turn
from lilac to mauve to burnt orange and then to indigo.

When parts of me diminish—I let them,
the end of the day is the end of me.

When I return in a new morning sky,
I have no memories from past cohesion—

I am a cloud, no thought, just float,
no care—just there.

REPAY

If Only We'd Known

I wasn't sure if we'd have that time again, so I travelled across the Channel and spent three days with you for your birthday. You were surprised that I stuck around, perhaps because I am normally in and out with the wind. We didn't do anything particularly interesting, just vegetated around each other, relishing in our old roles. There was no one to remind us almost twenty years had come and gone.

You tried to act indifferent, but I remember your face shining when my dog sat on the back of the sofa and wouldn't stop licking your ears—you smiled like the baby brother I remember in the photos and I felt a weird mix of sad and happy. When we were young, I wanted so desperately to be around you all of the time—you were my safe place.

Those three days were enough, and the last—you have a wife now and I'm growing a family on the other side of the world. Three days were enough to remember what age and experience has fragmented: who has dug a trench so deep into your heart, who you could never repay for all of the things they shouldn't have had to do, who knows more about you than you're comfortable with and who you will always love, even if they know exactly how to push your buttons.

FLOW

I've Decided to Give In

Is a crack born in a fissure of time—
was the Earth always made to bear them?

They have forged
tributaries under my skin,

water seeps out through my pores
to find its way back to the source.

I decide to give in—
stretch open and unencumbered,

my pain flows where form
knows no bounds.

I've never seen a crack in the ocean
and so I'm going there.

POSSIBLE

All That Loves You

And the wound that was not your wound
barely hurts any more.

The corner you were backed into
has crumbled into a wide open plain,

and you are doing things
that just weren't possible before.

You wonder whether this happened for you
to experience what it felt like to lose it all,

so that living was the only thing left for you to do—
the only thing that could be done,

for the sake of those you love—
and all that loves you.

TOWARD

In Ceremony With Yourself

It is okay to want to leave, even if the grief will crack them open like an egg and what is left will be too much for them to stomach. There are lovers who will be departed from—you do not have to hate something to move on. You don't always have to be going *against*. You can go toward. Bathe in your own light, dance to the vibration of your own drum—live in ceremony with *yourself*.

BLOOM

A Blaze of Light and Glory

I feel relief at the thought of returning—I have a strong sense that this is my last life. Which is so different from this morning, as I feebly sucked water through a straw with my legs above my head after fainting from the heat.

That won't be how I'll go—this star will implode in a blaze of light and glory. I'll be the mic drop on the stage in front of thousands after the best reprise of my life. Gold coins and roses will drop from the sky and my skin will absorb them, thorns and all. I will not bleed—I'll bloom. The road home will be a carnival parade of rainbow colours and I'll wave to everyone as they pass me by.

DECISION

Pieces of Ourselves in Others

Within every grand, life-changing decision are a million minuscule goodbyes. Mini-heartbreaks that crack like fine bone china, pieces of ourselves in others to try to fish out of the collective soup.

This beautiful new adventure means we are ships departing in opposite directions, we've been so good for each other we have blossomed. We've blossomed so beautifully the bees have carried us like pollen across opposite seas. I hope you feel the same warm sun on your skin wherever you are planted.

FORWARD

I Shall Die of an Enlarged Heart

I am off—embarking on the next train, never to look upon this land again. Autumn has had its season and now folds itself behind the horizon, giving up its seat to the Snow Moon whose swell mirrors my belly. The ghost I'm leaving behind—still a freshly baked memory.

They ask me with wide eyes if I am coming back and I cannot answer. Who could possibly know? I am prodded forward by life's turning hand with less to carry than I came here with. Perhaps when all of this is done, when I have nothing left to let go of, I shall die of an enlarged heart—too full to carry its own weight.

Am I sad to leave this place? There are no more whispers here, the land is silent. What lies in the new terrain? I hope we become wildly fast friends, two souls lost and now returned to one another. Motherhood—the meeting of the old self, the new self and the innocence—that which we carry forward like a cross to birth into new blossoming suns, hoping that this will be the world for them—that they will change it like they've changed us—from the inside out.

MEANING

I Want to Understand

Learning is all there can be now—you are gone—and if I don't learn something, why go at all? What was the point? Perhaps it's not about me and what I wanted, but what your soul came to do in the limited time you had. I want to understand—not why you're gone—but *the meaning of me still being here.*

Living With Loss (Acceptance & Hope)

Where there is sorrow there is holy ground
Oscar Wilde

Shortly after I moved to Canada with my husband, I attended an event at a studio called Rich and Grounded. I was stood by the snacks, as you do, and bumped into a non-assuming kindly faced woman. A natural conversation sparked up between us and it came to pass that she was clairvoyant and a Reiki Master. I was immediately intrigued and nervous at the same time. I felt this overwhelming sense of, *oh no, I'm going to learn something tonight I may not want to*. I had not intended to have an intuitive mediumship experience at all but as we were talking, a small voice was growing louder that this woman had something to tell me.

I paused and told her the feeling I was having and she smiled slightly, she said that it was best to ask myself properly if a session with her would be in the service of my highest good. She showed me how to tap into my intuition through the body. She told me to ask my body what 'yes' felt like for me and what no felt like. When I asked about 'yes', the weight in my body swung forward. I did the same with 'no', and I leaned instantly backwards. I felt at ease with her, she wasn't pushing me to part with my money, she was trying let me feel it out for myself. I posed the question whether this woman had something important to share with me. It was as if someone had pushed me so hard from behind, that I almost fell onto the floor. Her eyes widened and we promptly went into another room.

During the session, I closed my eyes and thought I saw an outline of a figure in the shapes of colour dancing across my eyes. The thought of my Dad popped into my mind and she immediately said, 'well, your dad is here'. I don't know why but I just knew he was and I didn't know how to feel about it. My relationship with my dad has always been complex. I didn't give anything away and waited for her to continue. She said she was starting to feel very woozy and dizzy, like she might throw up. I mentioned the alcohol and then she told me that he felt like he had to be tough and strong for the family, that he was so proud of me and that he admires his little granddaughter immensely. She told me she could see him tickling her chin and making her laugh right now. My dad then told the clairvoyant that he wanted me to pass a message onto my mum—that he was truly sorry for being so hard on her.

She asked me to pull three cards. The first said 'I am not dead', the second said 'I feel healthy and happy', and the last card felt really difficult to pull out, like there was an intense resistance to doing so. When I turned it over it said, 'Remember me by the happy memories we created'. This was difficult because every memory I have of him has been overshadowed by the fear and trauma. I didn't want to acknowledge the happy memories, perhaps as punishment, perhaps as a way to cling on to the story of my past. Ultimately, the main feeling I felt after hearing this, was relief. As much anger, resentment and pain I had towards my dad and his actions, it was melting away to hear that he had found peace and that he was sorry.

I felt like I could let that go now, that my dad was here for me and my daughter, showing up in a way that he never could when he was alive. Whatever our beliefs are regarding mediums or the afterlife, this moment is something I will always be so grateful for. After I finished the meeting I met my husband who showed me his phone immediately and laughed that our daughter was sitting in her chair laughing for no reason just before he left. I smiled and knew who it was, and that the medium had seen it too.

Even now, my daughter often sees something that I can't that she starts to talk, laugh and communicate with. I choose to think it's my dad, taking an active role in her life. This experience helped me to accept the past and move forward with hope for a better future, not just for me and my daughter, but for my loved ones now gone. I doubt I would have been ready to receive this message before it was truly time, and I'm so proud that after all of the grief around my dad I have carried for years, that I was brave enough to finally put it down without having to make sense of it.

Living with loss, although painful, means that our story continues—we not only get to experience the love and joys of life as well as the grief, but we deserve to. So before we delve in to the last cycle in the book, I want you to put your hand on your heart and repeat after me:

> *I take everything I have been through, everything I have learned and give thanks to myself for the perseverance and faith I have shown. I got here because I had the courage to meet my grief. My loved ones both here and gone are so proud of me.*

In the coming cycle, I encourage you to write what you needed to hear the most when you were devastated by loss, or when you were learning to live without the person or thing you loved so dearly. Write to your future self in case you forget how far you have come and need reminding of your resilience. Share what gave you the strength to carry on, or write to the loss or loved one thanking them for all you have learned. Give hope to those who are still shrouded by the black veil of grief, let them know that they aren't alone and that you understand. This is where your light is needed the most, so turn the page and let it shine.

BRIDGE

Who Would Have Thought?

Loss

a bridge to living

SHIELD

The Closest to Insanity

There is a new far-reaching separation when a woman begins to grow a heart in her womb, there are dangers and demons she must slay from within her own skin to save the life of a seed she can't see but knows with her entire body. She is alone because there is no one able to carry what she can. There are a million connections being made inside her with every breath and so the shield and sword is hers alone. Everyone and everything is a possible threat, there is no one to make absolutely sure of their survival apart from her own life.

No one talks about the grief of mothering without a mother. Now she has to make her own on behalf of someone else which is infinitely easier and excruciatingly more painful. She has to protect them, and even the word *family* does not excuse things any more. She has to protect them from her own family. Even when there is nobody to protect *her*.

Motherhood is the closest to insanity a woman will ever get— the most darkened you will see her, the most ravishingly strange and complex. She is part woman, part wolf and she grows sharp teeth, long claws and a sense of smell so strong she will hunt predators down for miles. She's prepared to lose herself in the making of her cub, and she howls herself hoarse at the moon—until they arrive on the first day of the sun.

Her body is no longer her own. It lives and breathes for them.

They pull her heartstrings and she must bend, she is their home now. Her arms will never just be arms, but the arms that hold them. As their chest rises and falls, and their lungs grow more powerful, they expand as parts of her minimise to make space— until the soft peach of a small cheek grows rotund from a smile. Her claws retract. She catches herself in the mirror—she is a tower of light, a warrior—a *mum*.

SURVIVED

If You Survive

Every one of you who survived, did so never knowing your tactics would save the lives of your comrades, the rookies not yet two months in, dropped into the middle of a battle they never signed up for.

The best leaders and heroes are the ones that spend their days trying not to be, and whilst they're unable to save those they love from a fate they haven't the power to alter—they are in the thick of it too, urging you through, because if you survive—you'll see that after *exists*.

SAFE

This Time

You're safe now,
she says,
and her words
form a string,
take on
their own life,
and fill my heart
with meaning.
This time,
I let the string
attach itself to me.

SOFT

I Owe All This to Grief

Devoid of sharp hooks
and jagged edges,
I've wept all solidity out of me—
my arms are a bed of feathers,
my voice as temporal as clouds
sliding across the sky.
My ear is as open as an orchid in bloom,
my footprint as subtle as a dewdrop
hanging from a leaf.
An easy life did not make me soft—
I owe all this to grief.

IMPERFECT

A Version of Recovery

However imperfect, we have this Summer to breathe again. To lie on the parched grass, wait for the answers to come, get bored and then go and find something else to do—like make salads as beautiful as a Monet painting, or watch the clouds undress and blush under our gaze.

We have this Summer to remind ourselves that we are the age we wished to be when we were young. That a bike ride is always a promise growing dust in our garages. We have this Summer to remind us that we aren't frozen lakes but ice-cream melting too fast to be eaten and that all seasons are a version of recovery—a wheel turning to open doors, as well as close them.

LIFT

I Have Done All I Can

I have watched loved ones
erode from the inside,
met death in the hollows
of their cheeks as the light
slowly faded from their eyes.

I have lain down my life
to ease their passing, which took
excruciating years to arrive.
I have offered warm hands,
gentle words, firm grit,
I have done what I can.

I have witnessed,
and watched over them—
and now I entrust you, Death,
to treat them with dignity. The same
that they showed in this life.
I have done all I can—and so
I lift them up towards your light.

DESTINY

My Last Breath

I've made a pact with the white butterflies that I shall make no impediment to their passing. I shall remain as restrained as a stone wall when they near and tickle my shoulders like they do when I'm bereft. If it is true that a butterfly is born as an echo of our loved ones last breath—they are spending their death giving new life and I won't be the reason they can't fulfil their destiny.

I will follow mine, let it all work out as promised—get out of the way of what was agreed long before I came. I will simply witness—until my last breath bears white wings and flutters towards the hearts of those left I've behind.

INDEX

An Assembly of Wild Nights

As you scroll your finger,
lightly brushing the index of my life—
what would define me?

I hope it is kindness and soul,
mysticism and magic, heart-lifter,
singer of songs that bring men home

to their mothers, and women
home to themselves.

I hope my book is long
and full of laughter, or short
and filled with rude jokes.

I hope *your* book is an assembly
of wild nights and passionate pastimes,
full of juicy mistakes

and hilarious attempts to avoid them.
I would read yours if I could,
but my book is closed—

which does not mean that I do not live,
that I cannot live on in your pages. I can—
if only you remember to write me down.

BEGINNINGS

The Reason Our Hearts Keep Beating

She tells me, she who is pocketed with loss and more whole than I've ever seen her—that when a child is lost during term or birth, their DNA lives on in our blood. We carry them as we carry on in spite of death, which means they are the reason our hearts keep beating. Every breath is also their breath. This is how the body heals itself, she says, as the garage light flickers on above her head, praising her in silver. This is how we make beginnings out of endings—we soak them into our very sinew until they are ready to try again. Until it is time to bear them.

TIDES

What Else Can You Do?

She always seems to stop me in my tracks—this wonderful and terrible life. As the years go by I've grown used to the vertigo, I've even become fond of her wry smile and wicked surprises. I've tried to avoid her so many times, spent my days trying to come up with a plan to put her on pause and its cost me years of living. Now I surf her like a wave, and move with the tides—what else can you do when you can't get off?

FLEETING

I Shall Linger

I shall inhale every flower I pass,
eat as many strawberries as my stomach will allow
and see you all one last time before I go.

I will travel on autumn's brown and orange
back to a place far away—too far to set a BBQ between us.
I shall linger on this sweet moment

and when I turn like the leaves and fall away,
I shall choose to be a wild dandelion blown apart
by the wind and scattered across this stunning Earth.

I shall greet each new horizon with the opening
of an eye and drink in the day. I shall grow under the dark soil
and bloom months or even years later—

just beyond that meadow, in the valley or beside the lake,
always offering something vibrant and beautiful—
however fragile and fleeting.

LIVING

Living Proof

Visit me at dawn and you'll see the back of my head leave my pillow. Meet me at noon and I'll be feeding myself and those I love, our bellies will not go hungry because of you. Challenge me in the evening and I won't stop the water from seeping through my pores and quenching the earth before the long stretch of tomorrow. Rouse me at dusk and I will thank you for all I have learned, for all that you gave me, one of those being absence. In return you have the latest splice of my soul to puzzle out. You've had me tired and depressed and desolate yet I've not stopped rising out of bed because I've not been living for you—I've been living as a metaphorical banner that says, *I am living proof that love outlives us.*

THANK

Undeveloped Photograph

Green grass, green heart—I'm an undeveloped photograph,
blessed with the opportunity to capture the moments
I've only dreamed of. To gather my faith like wildflowers,
and offer thanks to the dark—who brought her shadows
to show me the luminescence of my path.

RAINBOW

Nothing Will Ever be the Same

Nothing will ever be the same. I shall no longer call your name from the depths of my being—I will no longer barter and cajole, beg or persuade, I know you in the light and the shadow. I know where you hide and how to reveal you. I know how not to try to kill what you have already claimed. And if death is so sure of itself, then so too—is life.

I bet you never counted on that—the rainbow after the rain. You intensified but still I would not give up, my light a beacon in the depths of your black silk folds. I am the oxygen between two gates and I make my slow way from one to the other, giving life where I can.

Nothing will ever be the same, and I am glad.

READY

A Whisper In My Grandmother's Womb

I am ready to let death carry me,
to let it know best and see farther
than I ever could.

I am ready to release,
and what was once newborn
to grow into the old crone.

I have been melded down
in the furnace and poured into a mold
in the shape of a daughter.

I bow my head
to those who were chosen
long before I was a whisper

in my grandmother's womb.
I am ready to wield myself
with relentless love.

CHANGE

Everything Mattered Yet Nothing Did

So much can change with the drawing of breath,
with the day's slow clap and the tide's awesome stretch.

Families shrink and grow, lovers come and go,
new lands become home

and then you're back in the spare room
of your childhood friend's house,

whom you haven't seen in years
and everything is the same except it isn't—

the dog moves more slowly,
bed times have crept closer,

dialogue centres around babies
and glass jar collections.

There is a peace—
that everything mattered, yet nothing did.

The changes don't feel like a famine,
but a full basket of fruit brought home

to a field of faces whose eyes light up
when they see you coming.

REMEMBER

The Longest Road Home

May you experience love's tender refuge,
and the indomitable spirit that gives
your aching wings flight.

May you rest on love's tender shoulders
when you are tired and lost, finding comfort
in the caverns of compassion.

May you delight in love's laughter,
dance in harmony with the rhythms of life—
and know that your voice calls angels to their side.

May you be filled with imperishable light,
and as they walk the longest road home,
may your love be their guide.

AFTER

Where Wonder Lives

There are days when I wake up without scanning every part of my body for the wound. When my brain is no longer an angry rail passenger, screaming to get off and a morning walk is simply a walk and not a last ditch attempt to escape to somewhere between this realm and the next. There are days when I remember to eat breakfast and tasks are just that—tasks. When the bells toll at noon and I stop to listen as they sing their song of presence into my bones. There are days when I finally get to the mat and breathe beyond my trembling chest. When the breeze kisses my cheek and strokes my hair, when the park is alive with bees and birds, kids are climbing trees and nobody is harming each other. There are days when I touch the bark of trees and they feel like old friends speaking to me. When pockets of ease are known by my bones, when the weight of everything I cannot hold gives up on me—and my body that once felt like ice, melts and moves through the air like vapour. There will be a day for you too. I promise—*there is a life after this.*

PLANT YOUR GRIEF

* * *

LIVING WITH LOSS (ACCEPTANCE & HOPE)

* * *

Afterword

*If I die, survive me with such sheer force
that you waken the furies of the pallid and the cold*
Pablo Neruda

Wow, what a journey! You have shown up to the page and expressed yourself wholeheartedly. You felt the fear and doubt, and you did it anyway. I am so proud of you and I hope that you are proud of yourself. You are courageous and amazing.

This is an important time for some aftercare and I'd urge you to make time for this. Drink lots of water and get as much rest as you can within this next week, or for as long as you need. Delegate as much as possible at work or on household tasks to make some room for whatever wants to come next. This journey may have been something of a purge and there is a good chance that you will experience some physical or emotional shifts. You may also feel grounded, calm and full of gratitude. It is important to honour this too and to take time to receive that.

Burning sage or incense in the space that you often wrote in will help to clear any stagnant or stuck energy that was generated during this process. If this doesn't align with you, going for a swim, taking a long shower or initiating any other familiar rituals that signify cleansing or clearing for you will help. I often go to a park and find two trees that look like a doorway or a gate, I shed what I no longer want to carry and step forward between the trees into the life and the energy that I am claiming for myself. This external representation of what is going on internally does wonders for me personally.

You may want to mark this occasion with a celebration by taking your family out for a coffee and a treat, going on a solo trip, getting a massage or attending a comedy show. You may want to visit the grave or sacred place of your loved ones and thank them for supporting you throughout this time. Whatever it is, what you have just been through is a real moment and shows a perseverance that deserves to be marked in some way. If this seems too much right now, I understand. *I honour you anyway.*

If you don't feel 'better', or like you have only just opened up, this is normal. Everyone has their own timeline, sometimes the pain goes so deep that this may have only scratched the surface. This is still something. I've often found that things feel harder after healing at first, and so I encourage you to lean into it and trust that even though 'better' doesn't always feel pleasurable, you are being supported for your highest good and you are on the right path.

If you aren't quite sure what to do with all of the words that came spilling out of you, that's okay. You don't have to do anything with it. At least, you don't have to decide right now. Don't pressure yourself to share too early or to throw anything away. You will know what to do when the time comes, trust me. If you have any questions, please feel free to reach out to me on the Facebook group, or email me at a_poetontheroad@outlook.com—I'd love to connect with you.

Lastly I want to say a heartfelt *thank you*. Thank you for putting your faith in these prompts and for giving them your all. I can't tell you how much it means that our experiences have been transmuted onto paper and that parts of us have been healed or witnessed in ways we never thought possible. I am so grateful for you and I cherish you. Let us now honour the parts of us we had to leave to get here. Whoever you are—I hope this stunning poem by Emory Hall can offer you some closure and acceptance as we move forward within this messy and beautiful life, together.

AFTERWORD

make peace
with all the women
you once were.

lay flowers
at their feet.

offer them incense
and honey
and forgiveness.

honor them
and give them
your silence.

listen.

bless them
and let them be.

for they are the bones
of the temple
you sit in now.

for they are
the rivers
of wisdom
leading you toward
the sea.

— i have been a thousand different women

Emory Hall, — i have been a thousand different women from 'Made of Rivers'. Copyright 2024 Hay House LLC. Reprinted with permission from Emory Hall.

Acknowledgements

The highest reward for a person's toil is not what they get for it, but what they become by it
John Ruskin

A huge thanks to Jess, Daisy, and Amber for offering your incisive and professional eye on various sections within this book. You were all so generous with your time and attention and I'm forever grateful. Thank you to Emory Hall and Naomi Shihab Nye, for giving me a very prompt 'yes', for me to reprint your beautiful poems in this book—I am floored by your work and the essence that you bring to the world. To have your words printed next to mine is a dream come true. Thank you to Hay House LCC for supporting me with the formatting for Emory's poem — *i have been a thousand different women.*

Thank you to *Inkblots*, a wonderful writing group in Red Deer. You listened so patiently and generously whilst I read the first iteration of the introduction—long before it was ready to meet the world. Thank you for receiving my personal story with gentleness and understanding. You gave me the strength to share it further.

Thank you Mum, for giving me your blessing to share my story, I know it can't have been easy and I love you so much.

Patrick, my life partner, husband, and the best team member I've ever had the honour to work with. Where do I begin? Thank you for the safety and stability you provide, particularly during the creation of this book so that I could go to the places I needed to go to write it. Thank you for believing in me and showing absolute pride in my work. Thank you for telling everyone we meet about my books so I don't have to. Thank you for your part in gifting us our beautiful daughter Olivia, who is the reason why we do this. I could not have written any of my books without your unwavering love and support.

Olivia, every time I think this creative and unconventional life is too hard, and I want to follow the easy path, I look at you and know that this is bigger than just me. You give me the strength I need to carry on.

To Frank and Yvonne who took me in when I was five months pregnant so willingly and with so much love. You continue to do everything in your power to support your family, and we couldn't have done any of this without you. (Sorry for taking over your office, Frank!)

To all of the supportive spaces and community groups within Red Deer who champion the arts, thank you for welcoming me with open arms. *Writers Ink*, *Red Deer Arts Council*, *The Red Deer Public Library*, especially Lee who works tirelessly to offer free programs to support the literary arts. Thank you to Desiree at Rich and Grounded. Your studio was and is my sanctuary.

Your space feels like a temple where I go to remember who I am.

To all of the losses in my life, thank you. I wouldn't be where I am without you. Thank you for the lessons, for guiding and transforming me. Thank you to *Plant Your Grief* and the journey it took me on—for revealing parts of me that I never knew existed, stretching me beyond expectation and for delivering me home safely with an even stronger purpose and direction.

Professional Grief Support & Resources

United Kingdom (GB)

- **Cruse Bereavement Support** — National helpline for anyone grieving: 0808 808 1677; online & local services. cruse.org.uk
- **Child Bereavement UK** — Supports families with the loss of a child or when children grieve: 0800 02 888 40. pchildbereavementuk.org
- **Survivors of Bereavement by Suicide (SoBS)** — Peer-led support for adults bereaved by suicide: 0300 111 5065. uksobs.com
- **Marie Curie – Bereavement/Support Line** — Emotional support around terminal illness and bereavement: 0800 090 2309. mariecurie.org.uk
- **The Miscarriage Association** — Support for miscarriage, ectopic or molar pregnancy: 01924 200799. miscarriageassociation.org.uk
- **Nacoa (National Association for Children of Alcoholics)** — Helpline for those affected by parental drinking: 0800 358 3456. nacoa.org.uk

Northern Ireland

- **Lifeline (NI)** — 24/7 crisis helpline: 0808 808 8000. lifelinehelpline.info
- **Cruse Bereavement Support NI** — Bereavement support; helpline 0808 808 1677; cruse.org.uk
- **Northern Ireland Hospice – Bereavement Support** — One-to-one counselling for those bereaved through NI Hospice: 028 9078 1836. nihospice.org
- **Barnardo's NI – Child Bereavement Service** — Support for children & families: 028 9066 8333. barnardos.org.uk
- **SANDS Northern Ireland** — Support for baby loss (miscarriage, stillbirth): 0808 164 3332. sands.org.uk
- **Al-Anon Northern Ireland** — Support for families affected by someone else's drinking: 0800 0086 811. al-anonuk.org.uk

United States

- **988 Suicide & Crisis Lifeline** — Call or text 988 for 24/7 support. 988lifeline.org
- **Dougy Center** — Support for grieving children, teens & families: 503 775 5683. dougy.org
- **The Compassionate Friends** — Support for families after the loss of a loved one: 877-969-0010. compassionatefriends.org
- **AFSP – Suicide Loss Survivors** — Groups and resources for suicide bereavement. afsp.org
- **Share Pregnancy & Infant Loss Support** — For infant loss: 800-821-6819. nationalshare.org
- **Al-Anon Family Groups** — Support for those affected

by someone else's drinking: 1-888-425-2666. al-anon.org

Canada

- **Canada Suicide Crisis Helpline** (988) — Call or text 988 for 24/7 support. 988.ca
- **Kids Help Phone** — Youth support (5–25): 1-800-668-6868, text 686868. kidshelpphone.ca
- **Canadian Virtual Hospice** — Online grief resources and education. mygrief.ca
- **The Compassionate Friends Canada** — Support after the loss of a child: 1-866-823-0141. tcfcanada.net
- **Pregnancy & Infant Loss Support Centre (PILSC)** — Peer support & counselling: 1-825-205-7918. pilsc.org
- **Al-Anon Canada** — Support groups for families of alcoholics: 1-888-425-2666. al-anon.org

Asia

- **Samaritans of Singapore (SOS)** — 24/7 emotional support: +65 1800-221-4444. sos.org.sg
- **TELL Lifeline (Japan)** — English-language emotional support: +81 (0)3-5774-0992. telljp.com
- **SNEHA (India)** — Suicide prevention & emotional support: +91 44 2464 0050. snehaindia.org
- **Samaritan Befrienders Hong Kong** — Hotline for emotional support: +852 2389 2222. sbhk.org.hk
- **Little Angels (India)** — Support for miscarriage and stillbirth through peer groups and awareness: +91 9425 691 313. littleangelsindia.org
- **KELY Support Group (Hong Kong)** — Youth support for

substance issues: +852 2521 6890. kely.org

Australasia (Australia & New Zealand)

- **Griefline (Australia)** — Helpline & webchat: 1300 845 745. griefline.org.au
- **Australian Centre for Grief and Bereavement** — Specialist counselling: +61 3 9265 2100. grief.org.au
- **StandBy Support After Suicide** — 24/7 support: 1300 727 247. standbysupport.com.au
- **Red Nose Grief and Loss** — Baby and pregnancy loss: 1300 308 307. rednose.org.au
- **Turning Point (Australia)** — Addiction & family grief support: 1800 888 236. turningpoint.org.au

Europe

- **France – 3114** — National suicide prevention helpline: 31 14. Website: 3114.fr
- **Netherlands – 113 Zelfmoordpreventie** — Suicide prevention & bereavement: 0800 0113. Website 113.nl
- **Germany – TelefonSeelsorge** — 24/7 support lines: 0800 111 0 111 / 0800 111 0 222. telefonseelsorge.de
- **Ireland – Pieta** — Crisis and suicide bereavement support: 1800 247 247. pieta.ie
- **Association SPAMA (France)** — Perinatal bereavement (pregnancy/baby loss): +33 7 87 85 37 81. spama.asso.fr
- **Al-Anon Europe** — Peer support for families of alcoholics: see local contacts via al-anon.org

About the Author

Louise is an award-winning poet and performer, a bestselling author, and poetry course leader. She is originally from the UK and is now living in the province of Alberta in Canada.

Her debut book, *Plant Your Poetry: 365 Poems and Prompts to Grow Your Writing Habit* was published in April 2024, becoming one of Canada's most gifted poetry writing guides. She has facilitated poetry and creative writing workshops internationally and her words and poems have been published in multiple anthologies, magazines and journals around the world. Louise has been writing one poem a day for two years with a loyal following of writers from around the globe and offers daily prompts on her Substack. She is also the co-founder of Tandem Poets, a poetry collective elevating artist's work through co-authorship and collaboration.

If you have enjoyed this book and would like to connect with me further, you can subscribe to my Substack or follow me on Instagram for daily prompts, writing inspiration and insight. I'm always happy to respond to emails too at a_poetontheroad@outlook.com.

You can connect with me on:
- https://linktr.ee/a_poetontheroad
- https://www.facebook.com/poetontheroad
- https://www.instagram.com/a_poetontheroad

Subscribe to my newsletter:
- https://apoetontheroad.substack.com

Also by Louise Goodfield

Plant Your Poetry: 365 Poems and Prompts to Grow Your Writing Habit

Is the desire to write eating you up from the inside but you don't feel like a real writer and have no idea where to start? This book is for you! *Plant Your Poetry: 365 Poems and Prompts to Grow Your Writing Habit* is jam-packed with daily poetry prompts dedicated to helping you transform your writing life.

Guiding you every day for a year, the goal is simple: write on the prompt provided for ten minutes, without editing. Filled with lived experience and original poems by author and award-winning poet Louise Goodfield, watch your words blossom as you learn how to begin, keep going, and find your why for writing that will carry you through any challenges sent to test you.

This bestselling book is featured in critically acclaimed author Beth Kempton's Summer Writing Sanctuary 2024 (*Kokoro, Wabi Sabi, The Way of the Fearless Writer*)

Plant Your Love: 100 Poems and Prompts on Desire and Devotion

Part poetry collection, part creative guide, *Plant Your Love* is a heartfelt companion offering 100 poems and prompts to help you celebrate love in all its forms—romantic, platonic, quiet, wild, and everyday.

With personal stories and reflections on what gives love its lasting shape, these pages invite you to awaken gratitude, honour your heart's truth, and write with bold tenderness.

Whether you're writing for someone you adore, rekindling love for yourself, or simply noticing the beauty around you, *Plant Your Love* is an invitation to explore your desires, and let your heart speak.

Plant Your Love is due for release in January 2026.

Plant Your Joy: 100 Poems and Prompts on Presence and Wonder

Plant Your Joy is a playful invitation to notice what makes you come alive. Part poetry book, part creative spark, it offers 100 poems and prompts designed to wake up your senses and bring more wonder into the everyday.

This isn't about chasing happiness—it's about pausing long enough to see the golden moments already here: sunlight on your skin, laughter in the kitchen, the quiet thrill of being exactly where you are.

With tender personal stories and poetic nudges, this book invites you to write freely, feel deeply, and delight in your own presence. No rules. Just room to explore what joy means to you.

Whether you're in need of a fresh perspective or simply craving a little more light, *Plant Your Joy* offers daily reminders that the joy you're looking for might already be taking root—quiet, simple, and yours to notice.

Plant Your Joy is due for release in June 2026.

www.ingramcontent.com/pod-product-compliance
Lightning Source LLC
Chambersburg PA
CBHW042300030526
44119CB00066B/823